Advance praise for
What Pope Francis Really Said

"Pope Francis, like his namesake saint, is both loved and feared, despised and revered. Most of all, he is misunderstood and misinterpreted by conservatives and liberals alike. Tom Hoopes helps us see the Argentinian pope as he really is, and as we get to know him better we... see how Christ is working through one of his most powerful voices on earth."

—Fr. Dwight Longenecker, author, *Catholicism: Pure and Simple* and *The Romance of Religion*

"If you have ever been confused by press reports of what Pope Francis said about a particular issue, then you need to read *What Pope Francis Really Said*. Tom Hoopes identifies some of the most controversial statements attributed to Pope Francis and concisely provides the context needed to understand the true meaning of the Holy Father's remarks. "Part of the charm of Pope Francis is his openness to the media and his unguarded manner of expression. However, this style has sometimes left some committed Catholics scratching their heads. Tom Hoopes clears up much of the confusion caused by those seeking to twist the Holy Father's words for their own agenda. This is a must-read for anyone who wants to better understand the teaching of Pope Francis."

—The Most Rev. Joseph F. Naumann, Archbishop of Kansas City, Kansas

"Covering the inspired and at times confusing pronouncements of Pope Francis is not for the faint of heart. Tom Hoopes has boldly le~ the fray placing the pope's comments in context an⌐ discern the spiritual vision at play. This balan~ the mind of Pope Francis is so needed."

—Raym.

⌐a Over

"Pope Francis likes to talk and teach, and he especially seems to like departing from the script when he feels led to, and when he does, a free-for-all ensues. Boisterous voices from all sides cherry-pick a phrase here, a word there to give you their spin, until we all end up dizzy. Because this is true, *What Pope Francis Really Said: Words of Comfort and Challenge* is a timely gift. Working toward no agenda other than clarity, Hoopes takes a look at Pope Francis's biggest passions and most-quoted statements, and provides necessary context and light."

—Elizabeth Scalia, author, *Little Sins Mean a Lot*

"Hoopes has gone behind the headlines and the spin to uncover the wisdom and spiritual power of the real Pope Francis. This is the best one-volume explainer of the pope's sometimes disconcerting and surprising words, placing them in the contexts they so often lack in media reports. If you've ever wondered what Pope Francis really said, here is your go-to, one-stop source."

—Austen Ivereigh, author, *The Great Reformer: Francis and the Making of a Radical Pope*

WHAT POPE FRANCIS REALLY SAID

WORDS OF COMFORT AND CHALLENGE

TOM HOOPES

servant
AN IMPRINT OF
FRANCISCAN MEDIA
Cincinnati, Ohio

Cover and book design by Mark Sullivan
Cover image © Corbis | Ettore Ferrari

LIBRARY OF CONGRESS CATALOGING-IN-PUBLICATION DATA
Names: Hoopes, Tom, author.
Title: What Pope Francis really said : words of comfort and challenge / Tom Hoopes.
Description: Cincinnati : Servant, 2016. | Includes bibliographical references and index.
Identifiers: LCCN 2016027729 | ISBN 9781632530509 (trade paper : alk. paper)
Subjects: LCSH: Francis, Pope, 1936- | Catholic Church—Doctrines.
Classification: LCC BX1378.7 .H66 2016 | DDC 282.092—dc23
LC record available at https://lccn.loc.gov/2016027729

ISBN 978-1-63253-050-9

Published by Servant
an imprint of Franciscan Media
28 W. Liberty St.
Cincinnati, OH 45202
www.FranciscanMedia.org

Printed in the United States of America.
Printed on acid-free paper.
16 17 18 19 20   5 4 3 2 1

To my mom, who would have liked Pope Francis, to my dad who does, and to my "Pope Francis generation" sons and daughters, who should.

And to my fifth grade teacher, Mrs. Beers, to whom I have always planned to dedicate my first book.

CONTENTS

INTRODUCTION
Pope Francis: Up Close and Far Away ... ix

CHAPTER ONE
The Francis Option ... 1

CHAPTER TWO
The Golden Calf ... 11

CHAPTER THREE
Who Am I to Judge? ... 24

CHAPTER FOUR
The Peacemaker ... 37

CHAPTER FIVE
Welcoming the Unborn ... 49

CHAPTER SIX
Marriage, 2014–2015: Are Times a Changin'? ... 60

CHAPTER SEVEN
The Unity of the Church of Martyrs and Refugees ... 79

CHAPTER EIGHT
Big Green Problems ... 96

CHAPTER NINE
Land of the Free ... 110

CHAPTER TEN
Encounters with Francis ... 123

ACKNOWLEDGMENTS ... 133

NOTES ... 135

Pope Francis: Up Close and Far Away

Pope Francis is a mystery. He is reviled by some as too willing to change the Church and by others for being too stuck in antiquated doctrines. He is celebrated by some for saying things he never said and rejected by others for doing things that they don't really understand.

What you think of Pope Francis depends on what Pope Francis you have met. I discovered this when I compared my Fall 2013 to my daughter's.

She was a Benedictine College student on her semester abroad in Rome, on our campus in Florence, Italy. I was working at Benedictine College at its Kansas campus, writing articles for Catholic publications. Her fall semester was taken up with unfiltered encounters with Pope Francis that filled her with peace. My fall semester was taken up with vigorous defenses of Pope Francis amid media firestorms.

For some it had been a glorious summer; for others, it was the Autumn of Catholic Discontent—and both traced it to this son of Buenos Aires. The previous summer, the pope's "Who am I to judge?" comment about homosexuals had delighted the world, but caused a stir in some corners of the Church.

In September, the *America* magazine interview was published, and Catholics in the pro-life movement were hurt by the Holy Father's warnings against "small-minded rules" and being "obsessed with the transmission of a disjointed multitude of doctrines."

In November came Francis's Apostolic Exhortation *Evangelii Gaudium*, which repeated the pope's vigorous opposition to consumerist capitalism—and deeply worried defenders of capitalism. My Thanksgiving and Advent were taken up once again defending the pope…and worrying that I was getting sucked into a trap. "What if he really is as problematic as so many people say he is?"

Meanwhile, in St. Peter's Square, Cecilia was experiencing Pope Francis in an entirely different way. She sent pictures home of the pope interacting with the crowd right in front of her: Smiling and waving and making the sign of the cross, reaching down and blessing a little boy— and playfully turning the hat on his head. She returned to Rome when he consecrated the world to Our Lady of Fatima, and she sat for four hours in St. Peter's Square and prayed with the pope for peace in Syria. I looked up pictures of the event, hoping to spot her in the crowd. I never found her. Instead, I found photo after photo of Pope Francis standing in the half-light with a solemn face holding the Blessed Sacrament aloft in a beautiful monstrance.

"It was beautiful! So, so, so, so good," she texted, an uncharacteristic gush of emotion for her, but I couldn't tell what she was saying: Was it the pope's faith that was beautiful and good, or was it Jesus Christ in the Blessed Sacrament? "I don't know, but it changed my life," she said. A classmate who had strayed away from belief was with her that day. After encountering Francis, he wanted to dedicate his life to the Church.

She didn't overanalyze Pope Francis as a "liberal pope" or "conservative pope," a pastoral pope or doctrinal pope, a "Pauline pope" or "Petrine pope," as I was doing. She didn't seem to think much about him at all. She just sat there in the square and gazed with him at Jesus Christ.

It strikes me that my daughter and I have vastly different experiences of the Catholic Church. I grew up during a mass exodus of Catholics from the Church. Ours was the *People Adrift* Church Peter Steinfels described. Teachers, priests, and theologians were governed by what Msgr. Lorenzo Albacete called a "hermeneutic of suspicion," constantly doubting the faith, and constantly trying to update and improve on it.

Pope John Paul II waded in and began to stem the tide. Through his constant travels, he established islands of faith all over the world. With his World Youth Days, he almost single-handedly started a youth movement. His *Catechism of the Catholic Church* was truly a "universal catechism" that took the steam out of the dissent movement.

Cecilia grew up in the Church after John Paul's work was largely done. For us, the pope had been a rock in a storm; we clung to him for dear spiritual life as the torrents threatened to wash us away. For her, the storm was in the past and with it the desperation; the Rock of Peter was snow solid ground on a sunny day.

Pope Francis's faith is confident (like hers), not defensive (like mine). He took the bulletproof bubble off the pope-mobile and has called us to let our guard down, too. He doesn't want us to tiptoe through the world shivering at its darkness; he wants us to stride confidently into it, holding our lanterns high. He doesn't want to define sinners by their faults and exclude them; he wants to define them by grace and welcome them into the light to renew themselves. "This is pure Gospel," he says. "God is greater than sin."[1]

This book is an attempt to describe the Pope Francis Church that drew my daughter in: To see his Christ-centered vision and find our place in it. That work needs to be done now more than ever. In a remarkable confluence of events, many hot-button debates in the United States are going through a dramatic change at precisely the time when a remarkable new pope who speaks in a likeable, spontaneous, unguarded way has appeared on the scene. That means trouble in many ways, as we will see. But it also means a rare opportunity to communicate important truths to a world that thinks it has grown tired of listening to the Church but hasn't really even started.

All the old terms of debate seem to be changing. The way that we regard marriage and homosexuality as a society is completely different from how we did a decade ago. Immigration is literally changing the face of America, with traditional minority and majority categories projected to swap places by 2020. The anti-abortion movement has become the single biggest activist movement in America. Questions of war have been transformed by terrorism, our commitment to social justice faces a flood of immigrants, and questions of religious freedom in the West have been transformed by the alliance of market and government forces in a new health care regime.

It is into this crossroads that the Holy Spirit has given Pope Francis to the Church and the world.

UNDOING THE KNOTS OF MISUNDERSTANDING

In 1986, when Pope Francis was still just Father Jorge Bergoglio, an Argentinian Jesuit priest, he reintroduced an eighteenth century devotion that was little known outside of Germany and Austria until late in the twentieth century: Our Lady, Undoer or Knots—*Maria Knotenlöserin* in German. German emigrants to South America brought with them copies of the famous image of Mary busily working a knotted ribbon. When he discovered it as a student, the future Pope Francis loved the idea of Mary untangling the web of misunderstandings, hurt feelings, cross-purposes and false assumptions that plague human relationships.

To try to understand what Pope Francis wants from the Church in the twenty-first century, we should start by invoking Our Lady, Undoer of Knots. Our understanding of Pope Francis has become knotted up with conflicting feelings fed by mistaken reporting, false adulation, rash judgment, and the pope's own verbal slip-ups. To sort through it all, this book will take up the difficult issues he has raised in the order in which he raised them and try to loosen the tight knots we have made of them.

Providentially, looking at his pontificate in chronological order also allows us to examine his pontificate thematically.

First, we will look at what Pope Francis sees as the major problems preventing the world from having an encounter with Christ. The triple deity that the Golden Calf represents (the idolatry of money, sexual pleasure, and power) will get a chapter each—issues that he raised, in that order, in his first four months in office.

Second, we will look at how he sees the issues that have put the Church most in conflict with the world lately: abortion first, which he was accused of downplaying, and then marriage, which will fast-forward us through a two-year-long synod process up to his 2016 Post-Synodal Exhortation.

Third, we will see where his own priorities lie by looking at ecumenism, immigration, and the environment.

Finally, we will look at the effects of his 2015 visit to America. First, we will consider the surprising ways he engaged the issue of religious freedom in a secularized West and sum up his pastoral style through his signature "culture of encounter" approach for which he is so well known all over the world. In other words, we will end where my daughter began, no longer looking at Pope Francis from afar, but seeing him up close. My method throughout is to put Pope Francis as firmly as possible in the driver's seat, allowing him to speak for himself as we unravel the truth of what he has or hasn't said.

Mary, Undoer of Knots, pray for us!

CHAPTER ONE

The Francis Option

"Woman, you are set free of your infirmity."
—Luke 13:12

Cardinal Jorge Bergoglio's rise to the chair of Peter in March 2013 began with a four-minute speech in Rome.

In the days leading up to the conclave, the future Pope Francis addressed his brother cardinals, who were preparing to enter the conclave that would elect a new pope. His brief statement impressed them—with one impressed enough to ask the Argentinian cardinal for a copy of his remarks. What he got was a page of notes, little more than an outline, which is nonetheless a remarkable document: It carries in succinct, embryonic form the major themes that would shape the career of an enigmatic, surprising and tumultuous leadership style. In these brief remarks you see all the hallmarks of Francis: He is insistently centered on Jesus Christ, he quotes Pope Paul VI, and he calls the Church to go out to "the peripheries." You could call it the first articulation of "the Francis option."

"Put simply, there are two images of the Church," the future pope told the cardinals. There is the "Church which evangelizes and comes out of herself...and the worldly Church, living within herself, of herself, for herself."[1]

The speech fleshes out each image. The fruitful mother is a Marian image. Mary's faith is contemplative and active, both at once. She is the Virgin Mother of Jesus who presents her son to the world and presents the world to her son. She is the woman sweeping Elizabeth's kitchen, the guest noticing what is needed at the wedding at Cana, the central figure who sits among the apostles praying for the Holy Spirit after

Jesus's ascension. She is filled with youthful vigor regardless of her age because she is centered on others, and is filled with her son's urgent purpose.

"Thinking of the next pope," said Bergoglio, "he must be a man who, from the contemplation and adoration of Jesus Christ, helps the Church to go out to the existential peripheries, that helps her to be the fruitful mother, who gains life from 'the sweet and comforting joy of evangelizing.'"[2]

"When the Church does not come out of herself to evangelize, she becomes self-referential and then gets sick," he said. She becomes "the deformed woman of the Gospel."

The story in the Gospel of Luke goes like this:

> He was teaching in a synagogue on the sabbath. And a woman was there who for eighteen years had been crippled by a spirit; she was bent over, completely incapable of standing erect. When Jesus saw her, he called to her and said, "Woman, you are set free of your infirmity." He laid his hands on her, and she at once stood up straight and glorified God. (Luke 13:10–13)

But as so often happens in Jesus's life, that's not the end of the story. The leader of the synagogue is indignant that Jesus had cured her on the sabbath and uses the opportunity to publicly chide him, loudly telling the crowd: "There are six days when work should be done. Come on those days to be cured, not on the sabbath day" (Luke 13:14)

Jesus pushes back: "This daughter of Abraham, whom Satan has bound for eighteen years now, ought she not to have been set free on the sabbath day from this bondage?" (Luke 13:16). The synagogue official is humiliated, and the crowd rejoices (see Luke 13:14–17).

The story hits some of Pope Francis's favorite themes. It shows Jesus refusing to be stage-managed by what officialdom is asking him to do and instead turning his attention to those who are looking to have a real encounter with him. The villains in the story are the rules-bound religious men who have allowed a proscription of the law to take on a life of its own, away from its original purpose. It also sees the evil of a real, malignant, supernatural being as the heart of the problem. The Gospel tells us twice that her infirmity is more than physical: She is "crippled by a spirit," says Luke; "bound by Satan," says Jesus.

She is also the opposite of Mary, the vigorous woman at Christ's service. This woman is stuck in a defensive posture, a continual bow of automatic acquiescence to the world around her. Or perhaps she is too focused on herself, another constant theme of Francis: After all, you have to stoop to gaze at your navel. In either case, she is a kind of crooked doppelganger of the Church, carrying a bad spirit instead of the spirit of her son.

The Cardinal from Buenos Aires continued: "When the Church is self-referential, inadvertently, she believes she has her own light; she ceases to be the *mysterium lunae* [Latin, 'mystery of the moon,' i.e., reflecting the light of Christ the way the moon reflects the light of the sun] and gives way to that very serious evil, spiritual worldliness.... It lives to give glory only to one another."[3]

The cardinal was saying that the Church needed to contemplate Jesus Christ and model his eternal freshness to the world, not engage in endless self-analysis and stand before the world as a self-absorbed, neurotic relic of the past. The Church needed more than a rebranding, it needed a radical ("from the roots") renewal based in a deep faith in Jesus Christ. This is what Pope Francis wanted from the Church. What did the Church want from Pope Francis?

THREE POPES IN HISTORICAL CONTEXT

After the papal conclave in 2005, Chicago Cardinal Francis George gave the *Chicago Tribune* an insider's perspective, offering important context about what the cardinals were thinking when they elected previous popes. "Twenty-six years ago, when Karol Wojtyla was chosen to be the successor to Peter, some of the most difficult challenges to the Church's mission came from the East," Cardinal George said, referring to the Soviet Bloc that dominated world politics at the time. "Twenty-six years later, the most difficult challenges to the Church's mission come from the West. There is a man now [Pope Benedict XVI] very well-prepared who understands Western society and the history of the world."[4]

Popes tend to take after their namesakes. John Paul combined the mysticism of St. John the Evangelist, the beloved disciple who said, "God is love," with the no-nonsense focus on truth in action of St. Paul. He was the pope of love and truth, two principles that stood in fundamental opposition to the tide of statism and secularism that was at a high-water mark in the Soviet Bloc in Eastern Europe and continues to rise in the West.

The "love and truth" pontificate of Pope John Paul II seemed to go from strength to strength. He helped topple communist tyranny in the 1980s. He presided over a flowering of Catholic doctrine in the 1990s with the publication of the *Catechism*, *Ex Corde Ecclesiae* (his apostolic constitution for higher education), and encyclicals whose very names sum up the key elements missing from the intellectual life of our times and our Church: The Gospel of Life, The Splendor of Truth, and Faith and Reason.

Pope Benedict XVI was like his namesake St. Benedict, the founder of monasticism. You could sum up St. Benedict's contribution as "monks and manuscripts"; his Holy Rule translated the love of Christ into concrete practices of daily work and prayer that provided sisters and monks to the world, and his monasteries are famous for literally preserving the Church's teaching through the study and reproduction of important texts. Pope Benedict did the same thing: He gave the Church leaders and liturgy. Vatican watchers say Benedict spent his time focused on bishop appointees and the proper celebration of the Church's worship.

Winds of Change: The 2013 Conclave

The *Chicago Tribune* returned to Cardinal George in 2013 to ask about the election of Pope Francis. If Benedict had been elected to provide continuity with the "great papacy" of John Paul II, this time, the Church needed a new direction. At first, Cardinal George did not consider Cardinal Jorge Bergoglio a contender because the Argentinian prelate was seventy-six years old. But Bergoglio's address about the two images of the Church changed that. "It wasn't so much what he said as who said it and how he said it: very direct, very sincere," said Cardinal George. "He talked about the Church being a mission and not being self-referential, which is a wonderful thing to say."[5]

He said other cardinals had a similar message, but there was a difference about Cardinal Bergoglio. "It's not who is the holiest cardinal or who is the smartest. The most basic question is: Is he free to govern?" Cardinal George said. "He's free because he's a man of prayer. He's not attached to himself. He's internally free and externally free as much as possible."[6] Many of the 115 cardinals gathered in Rome apparently agreed. They entered the conclave in the Vatican on March 12, and white smoke emanating from the Sistine Chapel chimney signaled the election of a new pope the next day.

And how did Jorge Bergoglio choose his name? When it was clear that he was chosen, Pope Francis said his Brazilian friend, Cardinal Cláudio Hummes, "hugged [him], kissed [him] and said, 'Don't forget the poor.'" That comment inspired him to take the name of St. Francis of Assisi, who three days later he called "the man of poverty, the man of peace, the man who loves and protects creation"—three ways he would be described in the years to follow. [7]

The Chief of Sinners

But there is something else that Pope Francis and St. Francis have in common. The "freedom" Cardinal George saw in Bergoglio is reminiscent of the freedom of St. Francis, the saint who rejected the expectations and the path that society laid out for him and chose a life of poverty and preaching peace. In his *Life of Francis*, St. Bonaventure quotes the saint saying, "I think myself the chief of sinners."[8] The saint truly believed it, too. He said, "If Christ had shown as much mercy to the greatest criminal, I am convinced that he would be much more grateful to God than I."[9] Admitting you are a sinner is a very freeing experience. It frees you from having to keep up appearances, it frees you from having to be right all the time, it gives you the humility to be able to drop your own agenda and simply adopt Jesus Christ's. It is also the only honest self-assessment that a human being can have, so it frees you from illusions about yourself or others. And that makes seeing oneself as a sinner a prerequisite for being an effective pope.

Pope Francis says that he accepted his election with these words: "I am a sinner, but I trust in the infinite mercy and patience of our Lord Jesus Christ, and I accept in a spirit of penance."[10] To understand who Pope Francis is and where his missionary spirit comes from, you have to start with this self-description. Francis is not a superman, he is not an epic figure, he is not the incarnation of the Holy Spirit. He is an ordinary man who in his youth fell in love with the Jesus Christ, God made man, and has spent a lifetime fascinated by the Second Person of the Trinity, conversing with him and trying to mold himself into the man his creator intended for him to be. He sees himself first and foremost as a sinner in need of help—a deeply flawed human being who not only makes mistakes, but chooses what is wrong over what is right—and second, as a companion of Jesus, the Lord who is capable of working wonders in his disciples' lives.

EARLY SPIRITUAL INFLUENCES

Francis comes by this self-concept from his family in Argentina. He is a son of Italian immigrants who acquired his mother's love of cooking, his father's love of music, and his grandmother Rosa's deep and active faith. His sister describes the Buenos Aires household Jorge Bergoglio grew up in as a happy home with five children and not much money. Mr. Bergoglio was an accountant who played sports with his friends and sometimes brought his accounting ledgers home to work on while listening to Italian opera on the radio. Mrs. Bergoglio was a homemaker who learned on the job; an inexperienced cook as a young bride, she persevered in the kitchen until she could teach her newfound skill to her children.[11]

Jorge spent a lot of time at his grandparents' house, and it was his Grandma Rosa Bergoglio's influence that was decisive in Jorge's spiritual life. "It was my grandmother who taught me to pray," he told an Argentinian radio station. "She taught me a lot about faith and told me stories about the saints." A former Catholic Action speaker, she also taught him that followers of Jesus do not just enter into a private, personal relationship with the Lord: His love impels them to impact the world around them.[12]

NB

You can trace the basic trajectory of Jorge's love-relationship with Jesus in three separate encounters he had with the Lord. The first came at age seventeen in the confessional, locking in this understanding of himself as a sinner who Jesus loves. It is a sign of how profound the experience was for him that he remembers the date to this day: He was on his way to a Catholic Action meeting on September 21, 1954. As he was walking past the Basilica of St. Joseph in Buenos Aires, he had a sudden, irresistible inspiration to go to confession. In the sacraments, Catholics directly encounter Christ, acting through the priest. Jorge saw just how real that encounter is in the confessional that day. Years later, Bergoglio can't remember what he confessed, but he remembers realizing that Jesus Christ was calling him to follow him in the priesthood and knowing that he would obey.

"It was the surprise, the amazement of an encounter for which I realized I had been waiting," he told journalists when he was a bishop. "This is the religious experience: the amazement of meeting someone who is expecting you. From that moment on, God became for me the One who goes ahead of you. You are seeking him, and he seeks you first. You want to meet him, but he comes to meet you first."[13]

– Another flashpoint in the relationship of Francis and Jesus was the day Jorge Bergoglio became a priest. Grandma Rosa thought she might die before his ordination day—that "beautiful day on which you can hold in your consecrated hands Christ our Savior"—and wrote a kind of last testament and life direction for her grandson. He keeps her message in his breviary, which he uses every day to pray the psalms. Says the note:

> May these, my grandchildren, to whom I gave the best of my heart, have a long, happy life, but if someday sorrow, sickness, or the loss of a beloved person should fill them with distress, let them remember that a sigh directed toward the tabernacle, where the greatest and noblest martyr is, and a look at Mary at the foot of the Cross, can make a drop of balm fall on the deepest and most painful wounds.[14]

His grandmother pointed him to three pillars of his spirituality to this day: the Eucharist, Christ crucified, and the Blessed Virgin Mary.

– A third significant encounter involved his seeing Pope John Paul II in 1985 and helped cement his devotion to Mary and the rosary. Years later, he described what happened when he attended a rosary led by the pope, and gazed upon the Polish leader of the Church in prayer: "His witness struck me.... I understood the presence of Mary in the life of the pope.... From that time on I have recited the fifteen mysteries of the Rosary every day."[15]

These are the experiences that formed the identity of Francis such that the Vicar of Christ is also a companion of Christ. These encounters have played out in slow motion through his life, enriching and being enriched by his daily routine. In his landmark interview with *America* magazine in 2013, he described his daily prayer routine this way:

> I pray the breviary every morning. I like to pray with the psalms.

Then, later, I celebrate Mass. I pray the Rosary. What I really prefer is adoration in the evening, even when I get distracted and think of other things, or even fall asleep praying. In the evening then, between seven and eight o'clock, I stay in front of the Blessed Sacrament for an hour in adoration. But I pray mentally even when I am waiting at the dentist or at other times of the day.[16]

This is what a sinner does when he trusts the Lord: He talks to him, studies him, takes his cues from him in decisions he has to make, and tries to react to life's events the way Jesus would. And when a sinner does this, he finds peace, happiness and a fulfilling sense of purpose in his life. Then he wants to spread that peace, happiness, and purpose to as many people as he can. He becomes a missionary. To explain Pope Francis, you have to start with him, alone with Jesus Christ—and then watch how he shares that experience with others.

THE CHURCH THAT GOES OUT

What the cardinals saw in Pope Francis in that first brief talk before the conclave, the rest of us saw in his first homily. It, too, sounded almost like an outline, and it, too, was almost a manifesto of what was to come. "We can walk as much we want, we can build many things, but if we do not confess Jesus Christ, nothing will avail," he wrote. "We will become a pitiful NGO, but not the Church, the Bride of Christ."[17] He spent most of the homily insisting on the centrality of the crucified Christ:

> When one does not profess Jesus Christ—I recall the phrase of Leon Bloy—"Whoever does not pray to God, prays to the devil." When one does not profess Jesus Christ, one professes the worldliness of the devil.... When we walk without the Cross, when we build without the Cross, and when we profess Christ without the Cross, we are not disciples of the Lord. We are worldly, we are bishops, priests, cardinals, Popes, but not disciples of the Lord.[18]

Here again is Francis, the sinner focused on Jesus. We get a sense of the restlessness of Francis, anxious to get going, to get the Church on track, serving those who need her help most. But we also see an entirely new papal style, too: His words have not been carefully prepared; they don't cohere exactly into sentences the way they ought to. These are not the words of a man formed in the Vatican diplomatic corps; they are unpolished, extemporaneous, and heartfelt—the words of a busy pastor. Right away, we see how refreshing having an improvising pope can be—and how dangerous.

When I first read the homily, I instantly trusted Francis, but also instantly worried about Francis. I printed it out and took it to the theologians at Benedictine College in Kansas, where I work, to ask them what they thought about the line, "When one does not profess Jesus Christ, one professes the worldliness of the devil."

"Did the Holy Father just say that non-Christians are devil worshippers?" I asked. No, of course not, they said. He doesn't believe that. Then they uttered advice that many of us are still learning: "You have to read the line in context and not try to apply it elsewhere." No one had ever had to say that about the words of the former philosophy professor Pope John Paul II or the former theology professor Pope Benedict XVI. This was a new, unsettling experience: An imprecise pope given to hyperbole. We would get a lot of that in the years to come.

But the homily was exciting. It showed the boldness of Pope Francis and his vision of the Church. It was an honest Church, a Church of people who know they are sinners, just like everyone else in the world, and who know they need Jesus desperately, just like everyone else in the world.

CHAPTER TWO

The Golden Calf

"Woe to you who are rich!"
—Luke 6:24

Pope Francis is one of the most popular popes in memory for the same reason St. Francis is one the most popular saints of all time: He reminds us of Jesus. That was Cardinal Timothy Dolan's take when speaking to George Stephanopoulos on ABC's *This Week* on Pope Francis's first Easter Sunday. "Pope Francis.... Brings us back to the simplicity, the sincerity, just the raw basic goodness of the Gospel."[1]

And the world was watching. When his image was first broadcast, greeting the faithful from the balcony of St. Peter's, the new pope wore the traditional white cassock, leaving off the red satin cape trimmed in ermine fur that his predecessors wore. For ages, gold has been a symbol of riches; Pope Francis started a personal no-gold policy: No gold papal staff in his hand, no gold pectoral cross around his neck. He refused a gold papal ring, too, though he eventually agreed to gold plating.

Some of his gestures have been misconstrued by the press. By choosing to live in the Vatican guest house instead of the papal apartments, he said he was avoiding loneliness, not luxury.[2] He got a lot of credit for personally settling accounts with his previous lodgings in Rome after becoming Pope, but Pope Benedict XVI had done the same thing.[3] Pope Francis did not sneak out of the Vatican at night to help the homeless, as was rumored, but he did once invite the homeless to the Vatican museum. He dismissed as absurd the idea that the Vatican should sell off its ancient artwork, but he did raffle off Vatican gifts to serve the poor.

It is all part of Pope Francis's rebranding of the Church to look more like Jesus, who was poor, born in a manger, raised by a carpenter, and said, "Woe to you who are rich" (Luke 6:24).

A rebranding was needed. One much-shared Internet meme features a line-up of cardinals in an ornate Vatican chapel with the words "Vow of Poverty? You're doing it wrong." Another features Pope Benedict on an ornate chair with rich vestments, the image of a starving African child Photoshopped next to him. "What's wrong with this picture?" asks the caption.

In reality, though, the complaint about the Church's riches is misplaced. Yes, the artwork in the Vatican is worth a lot of money. But it would be no more appropriate to sell it than it would be to sell the National Archives. Vatican reporter John Allen adds valuable perspective to the exaggerated image of Vatican riches by comparing the Vatican's annual operating budget (less than $300 million) to Harvard University's ($3.7 billion), and the Vatican's $1 billion endowment to Harvard's $30.7 billion equivalent.[4]

Francis is helping the visuals match the reality.

"How I would like a poor church for the poor!" Francis told journalists on his first day as pope. On the following Holy Thursday, he followed up these words with his most dramatic—and controversial—act of embracing poverty.

The Holy Thursday evening Mass of the Last Supper is one of the chief celebrations of the Triduum, the high holy days that are the climax of the Catholic year. Before he died for our sins on Good Friday, Jesus ensured we would all have access to the graces of Easter Sunday by instituting the Eucharist and the priesthood. He began the Last Supper by washing the feet of his apostles as an example of love and service they were to follow and ended the celebration by giving them his body and blood under the signs of bread and wine.

It has been customary for popes to celebrate the Holy Thursday Mass at the Basilica of St. John Lateran, the cathedral of the bishop of Rome, and to wash the feet of twelve men, often priests. But days after his election, Pope Francis changed the plan. He celebrated the Mass of the Last Supper at the Casal del Marmo juvenile detention center in Rome and washed the feet of prisoners there—two of them women, including a young Muslim woman.[5] "It is the Lord's example," he told the prisoners. "He is the most important, and he washes feet, because with us what is highest must be at the service of others."[6]

The event sent shockwaves through the Church. The rubrics of the Mass call for men's feet to be washed. Popes follow rubrics or change them; they typically neither place themselves above the rubric nor model an attitude of disregard for them. It is true that the men-only foot washing rule had already been put aside by many bishops in the world. Christ's action on Holy Thursday has two dimensions: It is a teaching gesture about the institution of the priesthood, but it is also a sign that Jesus wants all of us to serve others. The original rubric emphasized the first interpretation. Bishops (for instance, in America in 1987) began emphasizing the second. So did Francis.

"Washing feet was important to present the Lord's spirit of service and love," said Father Federico Lombardi. "This community understands simple and essential things; they were not liturgy scholars."[7]

This was clearly the pope's intent: To speak to the world with his actions, much the way Jesus Christ did on the first Holy Thursday. That morning at the Chrism Mass, he had preached a homily introducing an image that captured what he believed to be an essential characteristic of the priesthood: "This I ask you," he said to priests, "be shepherds, with the 'smell of the sheep'; make it real, as shepherds among your flock, fishers of men."[8]

He also repeated language from his remark to cardinals before the conclave: "We need to 'go out,' then, in order to experience our own anointing, its power and its redemptive efficacy: to the 'outskirts' where there is suffering, bloodshed, blindness that longs for sight, and prisoners in thrall to many evil masters."[9]

Go out. Be real. Free the people from evil masters. These became watchwords in the pontificate of Pope Francis. And the images of Pope

Francis kissing the feet of juvenile offenders wearing T-shirts, jeans, and baggy shorts became icons that powerfully delivered that message all over the world.

IDOLATRY AND IDEOLOGY

"Look what he did on Thursday," Cardinal Dolan said on *ABC News.* "He is constantly reminding us that religion is not only about faith, what we believe…but it is also about how we live."[10]

After capturing the world's attention—and its imagination—Pope Francis used the first months of his papacy as a Catholic Living 101 course about what it means to be a Christian in the twenty-first century. He began his assault on the "three golden idols" in a May 16 address to ambassadors, tying our love of money to our great unhappiness. "We have created new idols," he said. "The worship of the golden calf of old has found a new and heartless image in the cult of money and the dictatorship of an economy which is faceless and lacking any truly humane goal."[11]

He sees this heartless cult as truly debasing. Francis called it a "gravely deficient human perspective, which reduces man to one of his needs alone, namely, consumption. Worse yet, human beings themselves are nowadays considered as consumer goods which can be used and thrown away."[12]

A few days later, on June 8, 2013, Pope Francis spoke to those participating in the "Ten Squares for Ten Commandments" initiative in Italy. In his remarks, Pope Francis said that the bibilical account of the ancient moral code and its first idolatrous lawbreakers is just as relevant today.[13]

"Recent history is marked by forms of tyranny, ideologies, types of logic that have imposed and oppressed and have not sought the good of people but, on the contrary, power, success, and profit." Against this, he said, "The Ten Commandments are a law of love…. True freedom is not that of following our own selfishness, our blind passions; rather it is that of loving, of choosing what is good in every situation."

What is Francis saying? Some context is in order.

The logic Pope Francis applies to the economy is the same logic a generation of American Catholics learned in the *Baltimore Catechism*:

Who is God? God is the Creator of heaven and earth, and of all things.

What is man? Man is a creature composed of body and soul, and made to the image and likeness of God.

Why did God make you? God made me to know Him, to love Him, and to serve Him in this world, and to be happy with Him forever in heaven.[14]

We were made *by God* to be *like God* and to be *with God*. The Ten Commandments were God's first great expression of what being like God looks like for us. In this way, the Ten Commandments don't enslave us to God: They free us from false masters and allow us to find our way to our true end. They were not meant to keep us in line so much as they were meant to keep us out of danger.

But Francis says the same problems that plagued the ancient Hebrews continue to plague us. "You shall not have not have strange gods before me," this First Commandment brought down from Mount Sinai, was immediately relevant to the Israelites. In Moses's absence, they had melted down all their gold, fashioned a bull calf out of it, and commenced dancing and revelry in celebration of their new god.

We would like to think we have advanced past that kind of silly display, but the whole thing sounds like it could be describing a typical music video. The symbol of the bull was clear: He was gold, literally made of money, he was virile, and he was powerful. In our day, the symbols may have changed, but our idols remain the same: money, power, and sex.

Why Idols Fail

We are built to worship. If we have faith in the real God who created the real world, our worship will lead us to the truth about ourselves. If we deny the true God, we will put something else in his place: an idol, and that will lead us to a lie about ourselves.

All idols will fail us. We will never have enough money to satisfy our desires, no matter how much we amass. Success disappears as easily as it comes; power is temporary and partial at best. Likewise, pleasure is fleeting. What is worse, when we follow an idol, we tend to recalibrate our worldview to fit our idol. The situation becomes what Francis calls "a seedbed for collective selfishness."

He described the effects in his encyclical *Laudato Si*:

> When people become self-centered and self-enclosed, their greed increases. The emptier a person's heart is, the more he or she needs things to buy, own and consume. It becomes almost impossible to accept the limits imposed by reality. In this horizon, a genuine sense of the common good also disappears.... Obsession with a consumerist lifestyle, above all when few people are capable of maintaining it, can only lead to violence and mutual destruction.[15]

We can see how this unspoken devotion to money in our own lives leads to destruction. We suffer from a condition Alasdair MacIntyre calls "heedlessness."[16] In today's "made in China" economy, we are rarely within six thousand miles of the people who made most of the nonfood items we buy in the store. We are also easily a thousand miles from those who grow our food. Those who pick and deliver the food are in lower socioeconomic classes that don't often interact with the middle class customers who enjoy the fruits of those labors.

But we rarely think of all the people whose hard lives make our quick and cheap shopping trips possible when we pick through the items at the local Walmart. It doesn't occur to us that we can only buy lettuce or tomatoes or bananas cheaply because somewhere else migrant agriculture workers are making barely enough money to survive. It doesn't occur to us that the toys, coolers, housewares, and smartphones we buy are affordable only because they were made by Chinese workers in conditions that would appall and outrage us if they were instituted in our own workplace.

Or maybe the thought has occurred to us: Maybe we have accepted that this is the way the world works now. We may even have celebrated it. After all, we might say, the system of free enterprise from the United States has brought unprecedented economic advancement to people all over the globe. In June 2013, *The Economist* published a study on the state of the world. "Nearly 1 billion people have been taken out of extreme poverty in 20 years," it said. "The world should aim to do the same again," it added, giving full credit to capitalism. The numbers it cited were impressive: "GDP per person" figures rose steadily world-wide through the twentieth century, and have continued to grow in the twenty-first century. There is no question that if you just look at economic numbers, the world is better off than it has been in a long time.[17]

But the numbers mask a darker reality. In China, millions of workers have to leave their hometowns and travel to work in the factories, often splitting up their families. There they find work, but with wages kept low in order to keep the prices down in America. No, they are not in grinding poverty anymore, but their families are not together anymore, either.

And while the West has brought economic gains to the world, it has also brought unprecedented moral degradation. At the dawn of the twenty-first century, St. John Paul II decried "the slavish conformity of cultures, or at least of key aspects of them, to cultural models deriving from the Western world." He said, "Western cultural models are enticing and alluring because of their remarkable scientific and technical cast, but regrettably there is growing evidence of their deepening human, spiritual and moral impoverishment."[18]

In the name of progress, we in the West have brought the world both greater economic opportunity—and greater exposure to pornography. We have exported jobs—but we have also exported aggressively secular film, television, and video game industries that supplant local cultures with the values of America's entertainment industry. The greatness of Pope Francis is that he refuses to be "heedless." He refuses to smile at the prosperity in one place that relies on poverty elsewhere, and he refuses to be dazzled by economic growth that brings moral decadence.

So Pope Francis has repeated again and again that the love of money is the definitive, destructive faith of our time. It wrecks communities in this life—and could lead to even worse in the next life by rejecting God's love.

"This love alone is the answer to that yearning for infinite happiness and love that we think we can satisfy with the idols of knowledge, power and riches," he said in his 2016 message for Lent. "Yet the danger always remains that by a constant refusal to open the doors of their hearts to Christ who knocks on them in the poor, the proud, rich and powerful will end up condemning themselves and plunging into the eternal abyss of solitude which is hell."[19]

POOR ECONOMICS?

This central, spiritual vision is at the heart of Pope Francis's economics. He is not just focused on bettering the material needs of the poor: He is focused on bettering the spiritual needs of rich and poor alike. But the full richness and depth of the pope's message about the idol of riches was lost on many in the West.

The pope's economic ideas started to get noticed at two points in his papacy. First was the publication of *Evangelii Gaudium* in his first September as pope. The letter was Francis's Magna Carta, a summing up of his plan to reach the world—but it also included a summary of what he thought had gone wrong.

In fact, Francis's understanding of slavery to materialism was the organizing principle of the document. The document introduces itself this way:

> The great danger in today's world, pervaded as it is by consumerism, is the desolation and anguish born of a complacent yet

covetous heart, the feverish pursuit of frivolous pleasures, and a blunted conscience. Whenever our interior life becomes caught up in its own interests and concerns, there is no longer room for others, no place for the poor. God's voice is no longer heard, the quiet joy of his love is no longer felt, and the desire to do good fades. This is a very real danger for believers too.[20]

Its section headings show how he applies this vision to economics:

"No to an economy of exclusion."

"No to the new idolatry of money."

"No to a financial system which rules rather than serves."

"No to the inequality which spawns violence."

The document was immediately misunderstood by two very different kinds of readers. At one extreme, Rush Limbaugh took to the airwaves to call the pope a Marxist.[21] At the other, atheist columnist Jonathan Freedland embraced the letter, calling for Francis to be a "pin-up on every liberal and leftist wall."[22]

But it wasn't until the 2015 publication of *Laudato Sí* that the reaction to Pope Francis's economic ideas became harsh and unrelenting: *National Review* titled its editorial "Laudato No."[23] At *The Federalist*, columnist Maureen Mullarkey called it "an extravagant rant."[24] David Brooks echoed their basic premise: The economic growth that had lifted so many from poverty in the past century would not have happened had Pope Francis's economic ideas held sway.[25]

It is worth asking: Had the pope overspiritualized economics? In his zeal to uproot idolatry, had he forgotten the good that money can, and must do? Had he, in fact, violated his own rule—was he no longer being real? In fact, the pope writes in *Laudato Sí*:

> In order to continue providing employment, it is imperative to promote an economy which favors productive diversity and business creativity. Business is a noble vocation, directed to producing wealth and improving our world. It can be a fruitful source of prosperity for the areas in which it operates, especially if it sees the

creation of jobs as an essential part of its service to the common good.[26]

Pope Francis knows the value of money and the necessity of business. But he wants it to be clear: the economy is for man, not the other way around, as economic ideologies would have it.

St. John Paul's *Centesimus Annus* (1991) spelled out our age's tendency to define people as dollar signs or social security numbers: "The individual today is often suffocated between two poles represented by the State and the marketplace," he writes. "At times it seems as though he exists only as a producer and consumer of goods, or as an object of State administration."[27] Given the choice between the state and market defining us, economic conservatives choose the market and economic liberals choose the state—but the popes choose none of the above.

In *Laudato Sí*, Pope Francis points out the flaws in each. "Politics and the economy tend to blame each other when it comes to poverty and environmental degradation," he writes. "While some are concerned only with financial gain, and others with holding on to or increasing their power, what we are left with are conflicts or spurious agreements where the last thing either party is concerned about is caring for the environment and protecting those who are most vulnerable."[28]

To Francis, those who see people as wallets and those who see them as pawns on the government's chessboard both wreak havoc on cultures. "A consumerist vision of human beings, encouraged by the mechanisms of today's globalized economy, has a levelling effect on cultures" as do "attempts to resolve all problems through uniform regulations."[29]

FOUR CAPITALIST SYSTEMS

Western eyes might read his critique of market excesses as a critique of capitalism—but we forget that capitalism is not a single monolithic system. In their book *Good Capitalism/Bad Capitalism*, William J. Baumol, Robert E. Litan, and Carl J. Schramm point out that there are four capitalist systems.

The first, *oligarchic capitalism*, is geared to patronage rather than lifting all boats. This was the capitalism Pope Francis saw in the class-divided Argentina, and he lived through the Great Depression that it caused in that country. Another is *state-guided capitalism*: Pope Francis warns that the perverse incentives in these societies tie the greed of politicians with corporate greed. This is the capitalism of China or Dubai—and, increasingly, the West, where as Alasdair MacIntyre put it, "What we confront today is a new leviathan: the state and market in a monstrous amalgam."[30] A third type of capitalism is *big-firm capitalism*, in which larger firms crowd out smaller ones—something that predominates in America.[31] In one of his strongest passages, Pope Francis points out how this undermines human freedom: "This paradigm leads people to believe that they are free as long as they have the supposed freedom to consume," he writes. "But those really free are the minority who wield economic and financial power."[32]

In *Good Capitalism/Bad Capitalism*, the authors' favorite is *entrepreneurial capitalism*, "in which large numbers of the actors within the economy not only have an unceasing drive and incentive to innovate but also undertake and commercialize radical or breakthrough innovations."[33] While the Church's social teaching chooses no system, this one shows the positive power of capitalism Pope Francis praises as "business creativity."

The old parable of the investment banker and the Mexican fisherman[34] sums up the "person-centered" economy Francis is always calling for. The story goes like this: An investment banker is vacationing in Mexico when he sees a fisherman pulling his boat onto shore in the late morning. "You fish for a living?" he asks. "Tell me, what's your typical day like?"

"I wake up late, fish a little, play with my children, and then take a siesta with my wife," he says. "In the evenings, I go into the village to see my friends, have a few drinks, play the guitar, and sing a few songs."

The investment banker scoffs and offers him some advice: "You should start by fishing longer every day. Catch and sell extra fish, and buy a bigger boat. More sales means more money, and you can keep adding trawlers until you have a fleet. Forget selling to the merchants in town. Get a contract with the processing plants in the city. Then you can leave this little village and move to Mexico City, Los Angeles, or even New York. In ten to twenty years you might even take your company public and make millions."

"And after that?" asks the fisherman.

"After that you'll be able to pay down your debt and hopefully retire and live the good life. If you work hard enough, maybe one day you will be able to afford to live in a tiny village near the coast, sleep late, play with your children, catch a few fish, take a siesta with your wife, and spend your evenings playing guitar and drinking with your friends!"

The punch line is funny, until you realize it's not. Which man's world would we rather live in? Which man's world *do* we live in? To fill out the story, you can imagine the throwaway culture the investment banker or the big-fish CEO would have to embrace to live his lifestyle: The international trips, the hotel stays, eating on the run, the damage to family relationships, and the relentless search for solace in entertainment.

Pope Francis does not reject capitalism. But he does reject a system where some get rich off of speculation while the middle class lives in a kind of wage-slavery to mortgage and credit card lenders, and both suffer epidemic levels of anxiety-related disorders—as they consume the cheap products an underclass of workers provide them at the cost of poisoned air and water in the Third World. And above all, he rejects the idolatry of money.

As Pope Francis's first encyclical *Lumen Fidei* spelled out in his first July, "Those who choose not to put their trust in God must hear the din of countless idols crying out: 'Put your trust in me!' Faith, tied as it is to conversion, is the opposite of idolatry; it breaks with idols to turn to the living God in a personal encounter," he wrote. "Herein lies the paradox: by constantly turning towards the Lord, we discover a sure path which liberates us from the dissolution imposed upon us by idols."[35]

Pope Francis thinks that what we need is to simplify our lifestyles and start anew with Christ. This is basic Christianity—Sermon on the Mount Christianity. How many of us, early in our relationship with Jesus, opened up the Gospels and became convicted by his powerful words about money? "Do not store up for yourselves treasures on earth, where moth and decay destroy, and thieves break in and steal. But store up treasures in heaven, where neither moth nor decay destroys, nor thieves break in and steal" (Matthew 6:19–20). Then, a few verses later: "No one can serve two masters. He will either hate one and love the other, or be devoted to one and despise the other. You cannot serve God and mammon" (6:24).

Pope Francis began his pontificate saying exactly that. It became a characteristic cry of the pope's in that first year, and ever since. That summer at the World Youth Day in Rio, he warned young people: "Nowadays, everyone, including our young people, feels attracted by the many idols which take the place of God and appear to offer hope: money, success, power, pleasure. Often a growing sense of loneliness and emptiness in the hearts of many people leads them to seek satisfaction in these ephemeral idols. Dear brothers and sisters, let us be lights of hope!"

CHAPTER THREE

"Who Am I to Judge?"

"Neither do I condemn you. Go and from now on
do not sin any more."
—John 8:11

If the world first defined Pope Francis by his personal simplicity and emphasis on the poor, it wasn't long before a second impression eclipsed it: His attitude toward homosexuality. On the plane ride back from World Youth Day in Rio de Janeiro, Pope Francis was interviewed by members of the press. As part of an answer to a question about a "gay lobby" in the Vatican, Pope Francis asked: "If someone is gay and is searching for the Lord and has good will, then who am I to judge him?"

The quote took on a life of its own. The magic five papal words were put in headlines worldwide. "Pope: 'Who am I to judge' gay people?" was the title of the story on *NBC News*.[1] Gay activist groups hailed the words and began to see Pope Francis as a potential ally. The phrase ended up on T-shirts, bumper stickers, and coffee mugs—sometimes in transformed images. One used an image of Jesus with the words "Gay Rights? Who am I to Judge?" One put the words in rainbow font between two rainbow-colored crucifixes.

Plenty of people demurred, however. Gay activist publications often struck a note of caution, pointing out that the pope had not changed Church doctrine in their favor and urging their readers to withhold support until he does. Many Catholic writers took offense at the pope's words. One friend of mine complained in an e-mail to me: "Who are you to judge? You're the pope! Judging the morality of behavior is your job description."

The quote seemed to have three effects on three different audiences. First, to gay activists who hoped for a softening of Church doctrine, it was a signal that change was in the air—and it depended on an individual's temperament how it was accepted. Optimists celebrated; pessimists wanted to wait to see what would follow it.

Second, to the general public and Catholics not well-versed in the Church's moral teachings, the quote gave the impression that his words changed everything. When the pope said, "Who am I to judge?" many (incorrectly) presumed he meant that there is nothing wrong with homosexual behavior.

Third, to Catholics who knew their faith well, the quote offered no new information at all. It is simply Church teaching that it is not our place to judge *anyone* who is seeking the Lord with good will.

Pope Francis himself explained what he was trying to say. In his landmark interview with *America* magazine, he said, "During the return flight from Rio de Janeiro I said that if a homosexual person is of good will and is in search of God, I am no one to judge. By saying this, I said what the *Catechism* says."[2] And what exactly does it say?

> The number of men and women who have deep-seated homosexual tendencies is not negligible. This inclination, which is objectively disordered, constitutes for most of them a trial. They must be accepted with respect, compassion, and sensitivity. Every sign of unjust discrimination in their regard should be avoided. These persons are called to fulfill God's will in their lives and, if they are Christians, to unite to the sacrifice of the Lord's Cross the difficulties they may encounter from their condition. (*CCC* 2358)

When the *Catechism* published in the 1990s, these words indeed represented a shift in tone for the Church. It was a transition from the days when homosexuality was "the love that dare not speak its name," as Oscar Wilde put it, or, more likely, the love that was called by the name of "pervert," "queer," or worse. Pope Francis seemed anxious to leave those days behind and remind us all that the Church does not prejudge anybody, but exists to welcome everybody into the way, truth, and life of Jesus Christ.

As he explained in *America*: "A person once asked me, in a provocative manner, if I approved of homosexuality. I replied with another question: 'Tell me: when God looks at a gay person, does he endorse the existence of this person with love, or reject and condemn this person?'"[3]

Once again, Pope Francis is taking his cue from Jesus Christ, who was once famously confronted by Pharisees who had caught a woman "in the very act" of adultery. "In the law, Moses commanded us to stone such women," they told him. "So what do you say?" First, Jesus said "Let the one among you who is without sin be the first to throw a stone at her." Then, when the bullies walked away, he said to the adulterer, "Woman, where are they? Has no one condemned you?... Neither do I condemn you. Go and from now on do not sin anymore" (John 8:1–11).

This has been the position of the Church all along, whose teachings build upon the foundation laid by Christ and the apostles. We are not supposed to define sinners by their sin and reject them; we are supposed to define sinners by their humanity and bring them to the God who heals them.

The problem with religious people is that we have not always been good at imitating Jesus in that story. All of us at one time or another has imitated the other characters in the story: the woman who sinned against God and others, or the judgmental Pharisees. Above all, we need humility to get it right and avoid proudly refusing sexual morality on the one hand, or proudly refusing to accept others' weaknesses on the other.

At the turn of the twenty-first century, there was clearly a widespread belief that homosexuals were victims and that the Catholic Church was on the side of the bullies. The culture came to this conclusion in part because it refused to admit that there are *any* sexual sins and in part because Catholics became too proud to accept others despite their sins.

The *Catechism* teaches that, while men and women with same-sex attraction are to be welcomed and accepted and loved, homosexual behavior is nonetheless still a sin:

Basing itself on Sacred Scripture, which presents homosexual acts as acts of grave depravity, tradition has always declared that "homosexual acts are intrinsically disordered." They are contrary to the natural law. They close the sexual act to the gift of life. They do not proceed from a genuine affective and sexual complementarity. Under no circumstances can they be approved.

If the world listens to that language and hears hate, or Phariseeism, it is because they have forgotten the Church's other teachings about sexual sin. The Church that refuses to condone homosexual behavior does not hate homosexuals any more than Jesus hated the woman caught in adultery just because he also said this: "From within people, from their hearts, come evil thoughts, unchastity, theft, murder, adultery, greed, malice, deceit, licentiousness, envy, blasphemy, arrogance, folly. All these evils come from within and they defile" (Mark 7:21–23).

There are many people for whom, according to Catholic moral teachings, romantic feelings can never lead to sexual intimacy. The Church does not hate any of them. Single people and even engaged couples are "barred from sex" by the Church—for a lifetime if they never marry. Even married couples are called upon to exercise self-control, sacrificing their own sexual desires out of love for their spouse, whether temporarily due to illness or separation, or permanently due to a physical or psychological impediment that arises after the wedding.

The Church's prohibition against sex, then, does not apply exclusively to homosexual sex, nor does the Church unfairly target a particular group of people who wish to express their love sexually outside of marriage. This won't console critics, but it should remind them that the Church is not discriminating in her teachings about homosexuality. She is consistently applying one constant teaching.

In his apostolic letter *Evangelii Gaudium*, Pope Francis noted how relativistic sexual attitudes are part of a vicious circle that shuts the Church out. "By completely rejecting the transcendent, [secular culture] has produced a growing deterioration of ethics, a weakening of the sense of personal and collective sin, and a steady increase in relativism," he said. As a result, the Church's teachings look unjust. When "moral relativism...is joined, not without inconsistency, to a belief in the absolute rights of individuals...the Church is perceived as promoting a particular prejudice and as interfering with individual freedom.'"[4]

Church teaching isn't an expression of hatred toward people engaged in homosexual sex acts any more than its teaching on contraception is an expression of hatred toward couples using contraception. Similarly, when the Church tells polygamists that they can't marry, the Church is not expressing hatred toward polygamists; it is expressing its commitment to a particular definition of marriage that the polygamist rejects. This same definition precludes gay couples from entering into marriage as well.

In fact, it was an act of love for Jesus to say to the woman caught in adultery not only "neither do I condemn you," but also, "go and do not sin anymore."

WHAT MARRIAGE IS

The confusion about hatred persists, however—and so does the confusion about Pope Francis's position. A vague sense that Pope Francis must be OK with homosexual behavior lingered from "Who am I to judge?" up to and including the 2014–2015 Synod on the Family. A later chapter will discuss the rumor that the synod would soften Church teaching about divorce. But in the fall of 2014, a different rumor arose in America: Pope Francis was going to accept the public commitment of noncelibate homosexuals as marriages.

But he would do no such thing. At a Vatican conference on the complementarity of men and women, he prayed that the colloquium would "be an inspiration to all who seek to support and strengthen the union of man and woman in marriage as a unique, natural, fundamental and beautiful good for persons, communities, and whole societies."[5]

He told African bishops, "Christian matrimony is a lifelong covenant of love between one man and one woman; it entails real sacrifices in order to turn away from illusory notions of sexual freedom and in order to foster conjugal fidelity."[6]

Together, these affirmations of the male/female complementarity being essential to marriage do not just show that the pope is opposed to homosexual marriage. They show that homosexual marriage does not even make sense as a concept, if you think of marriage, or sexuality, the way the pope and the Church does. In fact, he told the *La Nacion* newspaper, "Nobody mentioned homosexual marriage at the synod. It did not cross our minds!"[7]

Nor does gay marriage make sense if you think of marriage the way nearly every society and religion has throughout history. As Hillary Clinton put it in 2000, "Marriage has got historic, religious and moral content that goes back to the beginning of time and I think a marriage is as a marriage has always been, between a man and a woman."[8] And as Barack Obama put it in 2004, "Marriage is something sanctified between a man and a woman."[9]

Marriage has always been the institution society and the Church established to recognize, protect, and encourage childbearing relationships and child-rearing couples. It was never meant to be a government registry of sexual partners and was never merely a social affirmation of anyone's relationship. It was always a simple acknowledgment of what marriage represents: the start of a new family, for when a man and woman commit their lives to each other, babies naturally follow.

That is what makes heterosexual unions different from any other. They produce children, on their own, without intervention, sometimes even despite attempts to prevent it. The State is involved in marriage because marriage greatly increases the chances that the child will be raised in the best way possible—by the parents, in a team effort. The Church is involved in marriage because marriage greatly increases the chances that a couple will live in the most stable, moral way possible: In fidelity, through thick and thin to the end, in a love so powerful it brings new souls into the world.

As Sydney Archbishop Anthony Fisher put it: "Marriage has always been valued for holding together things that otherwise tend to pull apart: sex and love, love and babies, men and women, babies and parents. Not every marriage successfully unites all these things, but only the union of a man and woman can possibly do so."[10]

One reason the Church's teaching on the meaning of marriage strikes some as hateful or bigoted is that the connection between sex and babies has been severed. Because many Catholic couples have themselves rejected Church teaching on sex and are using contraception at roughly the same rate as the rest of the population, it looks for all the world like the Church is uniquely rejecting homosexual sex, when in fact, this is just one among other sexual behaviors rejected by the Church because they are closed to life.

As Pope Francis told one interviewer, the biological fact of a child-bearing relationship is vital to every marriage: "Openness to life is the condition of the Sacrament of Matrimony. A man cannot give the sacrament to the woman, and the woman give it to him, if they are not in agreement on this point, to be open to life."[11]

Why is this so important? The Church recognizes that sex has both "unitive and procreative" powers; it is a force driven by our need to connect and our need to reproduce. Sex that is open to life may be motivated by all kinds of conflicting desires, but what it is in its reality is a life-affirming imitation of God the Father, Son, and Holy Spirit, whose love generates more life, and therefore more love. Sex that is not open to life may also have good motives or bad—but it is always an act that is closed in on itself, an act from which no new life can emerge, an act that imitates not the exuberant self-giving of the living Trinity but the sterile stasis of an idol.

As Pope Francis put it in his 2016 exhortation on marriage: "The couple that loves and begets life is a true, living icon—not an idol like those of stone or gold prohibited by the Decalogue—capable of revealing God the Creator and Savior."[12]

In fact, just as we have fallen into an idolatrous relationship with money, we have also fallen into an idolatrous relationship with sexual pleasure. The more we keep money's value in our lives limited to its proper place, the more we enjoy our moderate means. The same with sex: The more we integrate it into a larger life that sees God in the first place, the more we enjoy a life in which sex is one detail of a bigger picture, not our defining feature.

SEX AND HUMAN DIGNITY

Pope Francis gave this advice to confessors in his book *The Name of God Is Mercy*: "I am glad we are talking about 'homosexual people' because before all else comes the individual person, in his wholeness and dignity. And people should not be defined only by their sexual tendencies: Let us not forget that God loves all his creatures and we are destined to receive his infinite love."[13]

Same-sex attracted people do not all identify themselves by their sexual identity. Far from it; many, many lead lives where their sexual dimension is simply a part of the whole person of who they are. On the other hand, some heterosexual people are prone to giving their sexual dimension a disproportionate place in their life and identity. Speaking to officials of the Rome diocese, Pope Francis said: "Each one of us can think in silence of people who live with no hope and are steeped in profound sadness from which they struggle to emerge, believing they have found happiness in alcohol, in drugs, in gambling, in the power of money, in sexuality unbridled by rules: However, they find themselves even more disappointed."[14]

One of the most common forms of sexual addiction is pornography, and it imprisons people regardless of their sexual preferences. In Africa, Pope Francis told young people where to turn for help: To their own country's martyrs who died rather than suffer sexual immorality.

"What would the Uganda martyrs say about the misuse of our modern means of communication, where young people are exposed to images and distorted views of sexuality that degrade human dignity, leading to sadness and emptiness?" he asked.[15]

Sexual fantasies are endless, sexual appetites are voracious, and sexual varieties are as limitless as the human imagination. That's why we have the faculty of reason and the guides our moral tradition gives us to sort them out and select the ones that will be a positive force in our life.

DARK SIDE OF THE FORCE

When marriage is no longer by definition an institution that promotes and protects childbearing couples, marriage ceases to be the basic building block of society, the bond keeping men and women together with their children. As a result, marriage loses its power as the force that makes each generation care more for the next generation than it does for itself.

Ultimately, any meddling with the purpose of marriage—including gay marriage, but also no-fault divorce, serial monogamy, and cohabitation —elevates the rights of individuals above the good of society. This turns God's gift into an idol of our own design.

While the damage done by widespread divorce is well known, details about gay marriage as a lived reality are only now emerging.

The New York Times reported in 2010 that homosexual marriage from the beginning was indeed redefining traditions and conventions more than anyone realized. "Gay nuptials are portrayed by opponents as an effort to rewrite the traditional rules of matrimony," wrote journalist Scott James. "Quietly, outside of the news media and courtroom spot-light, many gay couples are doing just that, according to groundbreaking new research."

He cited San Francisco State research that suggested that half of San Francisco's gay marriages became open relationships within their first three years. "The Gay Couples Study has followed 556 male couples for three years—about fifty percent of those surveyed have sex outside their relationships, with the knowledge and approval of their partners."[16]

In a January 2016 article in *The Daily Beast*, journalist Nico Lang said that the research wasn't a fluke. "Over the past decade and a half, studies from San Francisco State University and Alliant International University have found that around half of gay relationships are open," he wrote. "In a 2013 column for *Slate*, Hanna Rosin called non-monogamy the gay community's 'dirty little secret,' citing a study from the '80s, which showed that up to 82 percent of gay couples had sex with other people. That number sounds about right to me, but here's the thing: It's not dirty and it's hardly a secret, at least if you know where to look."[17]

This is why the Church guards marriage and the family. She has two millennia of experience and knows that new ways of doing it just don't work. The Catholic News Agency reported that at an October 14, 2014, in a question-and-answer session with members of the Schoenstatt movement, Pope Francis said the attempts to change the definition of marriage end up as an attack on the family.

"The family is being hit, the family is being struck and the family is being bastardized," he said. "What is being proposed is not marriage, it's an association. But it's not marriage! It's necessary to say these things very clearly and we have to say it!" he said, noting that "new forms" of unions are "totally destructive and limiting the greatness of the love of marriage."[18]

Harming the family means harming children. The gay activist website Homovox collected video testimonies of gay men speaking out against gay adoption. One gay man identified as Jean Pier said: "For me, the question behind this, the fundamental issue, is the child. Among the responses I've heard, I've had this business of freedom and equality. Then I pose this question: What of the freedom and equality of the child? The child won't have its equality vis-à-vis its friends in school. Its peers may have divorced and blended families, but they have, at least, a father and mother."

He said that he spoke from experience. "Twenty five years ago—remember, I'm forty-nine," he said, "like everyone else, I wanted to have a child; it was a question of transmitting my heritage. But then I realized very quickly that if I were going to have a child that way, it would be for the wrong reasons."[19]

I personally interviewed homosexual activist John McKellar in 2002. At the time, he was president of Homosexuals Opposed to Pride Extremism (HOPE). He also opposed gay adoption. "Sure, we all have baby envy, and lots of us would like to raise kids," he said. "But we can't have everything we want in life, and it's selfish and rude to redefine society's traditions and conventions simply for our self-indulgence."[20]

Pope Francis also has children in mind when he opposes what he calls "ideological colonization" of "gender theory" ideas. In an airplane interview on his trip back to Rome from the Philippines he told the story of an education official in Latin America who was offered a needed loan to build schools for the poor—provided the children be taught from a particular book. "It was a school book, a well-thought-out book, pedagogically speaking, in which gender theory was taught.... This is ideological colonization.... They colonize the people with an idea which changes, or means to change, a mentality or a structure."[21]

He compared this "ideological colonization" to dictatorships that try to brainwash a people from childhood in the theories of their masters, calling the Hitler Youth an example of the phenomenon.

He reprised that theme in a discussion with the Diocese of Rome that summer. Secular media reports pointed out that his words came a day after a major gay pride march in Rome, but the pope didn't seem to have that on his mind. He was speaking of the complementarity of husband and wife, and said, "What great richness this diversity is; a diversity which becomes complementary.... Children mature seeing their father and mother like this; their identity matures being confronted with the love their father and mother have, confronted with this difference." And he once again warned families to stand up to "ideological colonizations that poison the soul."[22]

In his 2016 document on the family, he argued that both gender ideology and same-sex marriage undermine marriage and therefore society.

"We need to acknowledge the great variety of family situations that can offer a certain stability, but de facto or same-sex unions, for example, may not simply be equated with marriage. No union that is temporary or closed to the transmission of life can ensure the future of society," he wrote. "Yet another challenge is posed by the various forms of an ideology of gender that 'denies the difference and reciprocity in nature of a man and a woman and envisages a society without sexual differences, thereby eliminating the anthropological basis of the family.'"[23]

THE CHRISTIAN PARADOX

And so it is that the homosexual issue illustrates perfectly the Christian paradox of Pope Francis. The paradox of Francis is the paradox of the Gospel. He can see with absolute clarity the great value of homosexual men and women and at the same time he can see the great danger to our society that homosexual marriage will bring.

He is particularly worried that children who experience same-sex attraction not be rejected. He told *La Nacion* newspaper that the Synod addressed "how a family with a homosexual child, whether a son or a daughter, goes about educating that child, how the family bears up, how to help that family to deal with that somewhat unusual situation.... We have to find a way to help that father or that mother to stand by their son or daughter."[24]

Just as he made an impression by washing the feet of Muslim woman prisoner on his first Holy Thursday as pope—he made an impression on his first Holy Thursday Mass as archbishop, too. Austen Ivereigh tells the story in his book *The Great Reformer*.

Bergoglio called the chaplain of the Muñiz Hospital in Buenos Aires—the national center for the treatment of infectious conditions—and asked if he could say the Holy Thursday Mass there.... When the archbishop arrived, Father Andrés Tello explained that eight of ten of the patients had AIDS; they had an average age of twenty-eight; many were drug addicts or prostitutes; some were transgender. I told him that while the Gospel talks about twelve male apostles, here we had men and women as well as transvestites, but he said: "you choose them, I'll wash their feet." ... The Mass was very emotional. Everyone was in tears.[25]

Again and again we hear of Pope Francis's encounters with homosexual men and women, transvestites, and transsexuals. He doesn't avoid them just as he doesn't avoid the rest of us; we are sinners too. He is not just like Jesus Christ denouncing sexual sin. He is also like Jesus Christ touching the sinner with healing hands and saying, "Neither do I condemn you. Go and do not sin anymore."

CHAPTER FOUR

The Peacemaker

"You have heard that it was said, 'You shall love your neighbor and hate
your enemy.' But I say to you, love your enemies."
—Matthew 5:43–44

If the pope were a politician, you would have said he had big momentum
after that first summer of 2013.

In July, World Youth Day 2013 in Rio de Janeiro was an unquali-
fied triumph. "I think history will show that World Youth Day in Brazil
was one of the most successful of all World Youth Days," said Bishop
Conley of Lincoln, Nebraska. He was struck by the number of people
who stopped him in the streets and asked for a blessing. "They loved the
fact that their shepherds were in the streets, walking with the people."[1]

The bishop and the popes were going out into the streets, and the
people were responding. On July 26, at one point a nine-year-old
Brazilian in a soccer jersey broke past barriers to deliver a message to
Pope Francis. "Your Holiness, I want to be a priest of Christ, a represen-
tative of Christ," he said. The pope, in tears, asked him to pray for him
and said, "As of today, your vocation is set."[2]

Young pilgrims from across the United States told reporters that they
had been drifting from the faith, but after their encounter with Pope
Francis amid a sea of young faces, they were ready to take on the world.[3]
"All I thought was that we are not alone here. There are more of us.
When we saw the pope and I heard his speech I teared up a little because
to me all he said was the truth," said one young American pilgrim.[4]

"I had the blessing of seeing Pope Francis up so close," said another.
"His face beamed with happiness, and it was there that I realized he
wasn't joking when he said we were capable of going out and making
disciples of all nations."[5]

Pilgrims describe how, at a nighttime prayer vigil on Copacabana Beach the night before the final Mass, the rhythm of the waves melded powerfully with the hymns and the voice of the Holy Father. "Dear young people, please, don't be observers of life, but get involved," Pope Francis told them. "Jesus did not remain an observer, but he immersed himself. Don't be observers, but immerse yourself in the reality of life, as Jesus did."[6]

Because a planned campsite had been flooded with water, many of the young people had nowhere to go, and so they stayed on the beach overnight.

Bishop Conley remembered the scene the next morning. "The sun rose over Copacabana Beach Sunday morning, and three million young people assembled along the water's edge," he said. "Most of those three million pilgrims had spent the night on the beach."

In his homily at that Mass, Pope Francis invited the world's young Catholics to share his vision. "Do not be afraid to go and to bring Christ into every area of life, to the fringes of society, even to those who seem farthest away, most indifferent," he said.[7]

His words had a powerful impact—but pilgrims were just as struck by his example. Katherine Bauman, a Benedictine College student at the time, presented the first reading at the Mass. She told me what it was like to see Pope Francis up close:

> I was particularly struck by his simplicity, his humanity.... He is one of the biggest 'celebrities' in the world, and it is clear that he hates the attention, yet he is radiant with joy when he is driven through the crowds. It is obvious that the excitement is not because he is in the spotlight—he does not see crowds, but people, persons, God's children, and he loves each one of them for that. He is a living example of his own call to truly encounter others, and his demeanor reminds me of the simplicity and accessibility of Christ in his humanity.[8]

SEEING PEACE

The pope's five-hour vigil for peace in Syria had the same effect on those who were there. I have described my daughter's experience there, but it was her first exposure to such a thing. You would expect her to be impressed. You wouldn't necessarily expect it from Father Federico Lombardi. He started working in the Vatican when John Paul II was less than halfway through his papacy.

"I've been here for 23 years," said the papal spokesman, "and I remember gatherings for peace in Assisi, but I don't remember anything with this dimension in St. Peter's Square."[9]

The vigil for peace in Syria was born in the last two weeks of August 2013, when heartbreaking photographs started appearing in the news: Rows of corpses of men, women, and children laid out in white cotton body bags. *The New York Times* reported on the "telltale signs of chemical weapons": "corpses without visible injury; hospitals flooded with victims, gasping for breath, trembling and staring ahead languidly; images of a gray cloud bursting over a neighborhood."[10] By August 30, *The Washington Post* was reporting that more than 1,400 people had been killed in chemical weapons attacks by the Syrian government targeting rebels in the nation's civil war.[11]

On September 1, 2013, Pope Francis used his Sunday Angelus remarks to register his horror. "Those terrible images from recent days are burned into my mind and heart," he said. "There is the judgment of God, and also the judgment of history, upon our actions from which there is no escaping."[12] Then, he delivered a message to the West with an uncharacteristic shout: "War brings on war! Violence brings on violence!"

Pope Francis announced a worldwide day of fasting and prayer for peace to be marked with a vigil in St. Peter's Square set for Saturday, September 7. Churches worldwide held their own vigils in solidarity with the pope. The Archdiocese of Madrid devoted all the day's Masses to the intention of peace in Syria and citywide, church bells rang out at noon to call Catholics to pray an Angelus dedicated to Mary, Queen of Peace. Cardinal Timothy Dolan, the Archbishop of New York, said a Mass for peace in Syria at the cathedral and asked Catholics to abstain from meat as a fast for the intention. The Archdiocese of Denver offered adoration from 7:00 PM until midnight, joining in the prayers for peace.

But in Rome, the pilgrims came from all over, pouring out of trains and buses to get to the Vatican. Americans rearranged their European vacations to be there. When the prayer vigil started, religious sisters and seminarians filled St. Peter's Square, but so did mothers with their infants in their arms, locals, and men and women of every nationality.

Pilgrims told reporters how deeply moving the event was. A Minnesotan man whose family was practically trapped by the event on a vacation stop at the Vatican museums said he felt a "sense of peace and the oneness of humanity" in St. Peter's Square that he hoped could "resonate with all of the leaders of the world."[13]

An Italian pilgrim said, "Today is a very important day. Pope Francis's voice is very powerful. Not only Christians but Muslims and Jewish people and non-believers listen to his word. Maybe new ways of peace are coming."[14]

Pope Francis's prayer vigil started with dozens of priests offering confessions starting at 5:45 that morning. After readings and prayers, four Swiss Guards carried a statue of Mary, Protectress of the Roman People, through the square, with two girls spreading flowers before them. The Holy Father led the rosary, invoking Our Lady, Queen of Peace, with each mystery. There followed readings and prayers climaxing in an extended silent period of Eucharistic Adoration scheduled to begin that morning at 10:15.

At that event, Francis spelled out his vision of war and peace in a dramatic, succinct way. Violence came from the same source as greed and sexual immorality: Idolatry. In his meditation, he told the pilgrims: "When man thinks only of himself, of his own interests and places himself in the center, when he permits himself to be captivated by the idols of dominion and power, when he puts himself in God's place, then all relationships are broken and everything is ruined; then the door opens to violence, indifference, and conflict."[15]

The pope sees the origins of war in the origins of mankind.

"God asks man's conscience: 'Where is Abel your brother?' and Cain responds: 'I do not know; am I my brother's keeper?'" he said. "We too are asked this question, it would be good for us to ask ourselves as well: Am I really my brother's keeper? Yes, you are your brother's keeper!"

He said that we "bring about the rebirth of Cain with every act of violence" but that it doesn't have to be this way. If Cain was an icon of a sinner hardened in his corruption, Jesus Christ crucified is an icon of how far God will go to free sinners from slavery to evil.

"My Christian faith urges me to look to the Cross," said the pope. "There, we can see God's reply: violence is not answered with violence, death is not answered with the language of death. In the silence of the Cross, the uproar of weapons ceases and the language of reconciliation, forgiveness, dialogue, and peace is spoken."

Before leaving the pilgrims in silence before the real presence of Jesus Christ in the Eucharist, he offered a little examination of conscience and a resolution:

> Is it possible to walk the path of peace? Can we get out of this spiral of sorrow and death? Can we learn once again to walk and live in the ways of peace?" he asked. "Invoking the help of God, under the maternal gaze of the Salus Populi Romani, Queen of Peace, I say: Yes, it is possible for everyone! From every corner of the world tonight, I would like to hear us cry out: Yes, it is possible for everyone! Or even better, I would like for each one of us, from the least to the greatest, including those called to govern nations, to respond: Yes, we want it!

He would turn to the same themes again and again when he spoke about war: personal conversion, the cross, a new fraternity of man. When the angels declared, "Peace on earth and good will to men," at Christ's birth, they didn't mean that now, God would magically end war: They meant that he would teach human beings, through Christ, how to live lives reconciled with God and each other—and that we Christians would bring peace on earth by the way we live.

The vigil had a profound effect worldwide. People watched in astonishment in the days that followed it as Syria's leaders handed over their chemical weapons without military intervention. Whether that was an answer to prayer or a reaction to Pope Francis's forceful cry for peace or just a happy coincidence, it strengthened the reputation of Francis, the peacemaker. But for some of those who sat in St. Peter's Square, the transformative effect was powerful, personal, and permanent.[16]

THE RESCUED AND THE RESCUERS

Once again, the pope was offering a lesson in Catholicism 101. Much of Francis's call for peace was a paraphrase from the *Catechism*: "All citizens and all governments are obliged to work for the avoidance of war." It is a lesson Americans needed to hear. But for many Americans, this call to end war and live in a brotherhood of love and peace sounds idealistic and unrealistic. In fact, in an age of well-armed terrorists, rogue nations seeking nuclear weapons and a proliferation of Syria-style chemical weapons, Pope Francis's words might even sound dangerous. If we ever had the luxury of indulging in wishful thinking about peace, we certainly don't now.

This difference in perspective between Americans and much of the rest of the world comes from our culture and our history. Americans have a healthy appreciation for military virtues. We call our military men and women heroes and applaud them at public events because we recognize in them virtues that we lack. "No one has greater love than this," said Jesus, "to lay down one's life for one's friends."

Our veterans have lived that verse literally—not just in battle, but in the way they gave their lives to a system like that described by the military leader who Jesus praises in the Gospel, the centurion. "For I too am a person subject to authority, with soldiers subject to me," he tells Jesus. "And I say to one, 'Go,' and he goes; and to another, 'Come here,' and he comes" (Luke 7:8). In the twenty-first century, the military has preserved the virtues of discipline, hard work, and loyalty beyond partisanship that are the antithesis of the carelessness and lack of discipline that too many of us have given into.

When Americans think of war, we think of our military rushing to the aid of the downtrodden: the victims of the Taliban or Saddam Hussein or the Nazis. To hear the pope say that war is always wrong and that violence always leads to violence sounds not just idealistic but factually incorrect. Would you tell the survivors of the concentration camps that war is never good?

Actually, World War II is an example our most recent popes have often used of how war is sometimes necessary—but never desirable. The Church's age-old just war theory spells out the conditions under which military action is warranted. Pope Francis gave his own take on the just war rules on his flight to Korea from Rome in 2014. Paraphrasing the *Catechism* (2309), he said, "In these cases, where there is an unjust aggression, I can only say that it is licit to stop the unjust aggressor. I emphasize the word: 'stop'. I'm not saying drop bombs, make war, but stop the aggressor."[17]

The way the *Catechism* puts it is that "the damage inflicted by the aggressor on the nation or community of nations must be lasting, grave, and certain." Pope Francis argued that a threat to the community of nations has to be established by a community of nations. "One nation alone cannot determine how to stop an unjust aggressor. After World War II, there was the idea of the United Nations: that is where discussion was to take place, to say: Is this an unjust aggressor? It would seem so. How do we stop him?' This alone, nothing else."[18]

The pope added that just war is not just permissible, but sometimes it is absolutely necessary. "To stop an unjust aggressor is a right of humanity, but it is also a right of the aggressor to be stopped in order not to do evil." The principle is the same as it is with an individual's right to self-defense: Christians never want to kill. If the only way to save a life is to use deadly force, the Christian will resort to it as a saving act, not as a deadly one.

But even in the situation where a just war must be waged, Pope Francis still warned about the siren song of the idol power. "How many times, with this excuse of stopping an unjust aggressor, the powers have taken over peoples and carried on an actual war of conquest!" he said.

Americans have one view of World War II; Europeans have another. We all agree it was a just war, but the point of view of the rescuer is different from that of the rescued. For St. John Paul II, World War II was the time that his native Poland was overtaken by the Nazis, turning neighbor against neighbor and taking many neighbors away forever. When he was Archbishop of Krakow, Liberation Day from the Nazis was a Polish national holiday because the new Soviet occupiers mandated it.

Or think of Pope Benedict XVI. American families were opposed to the Nazis and sent their children far away to fight them; Pope Benedict's family, the Ratzingers, also opposed the Nazis, but had to watch helplessly as their children's names were added to lists of Hitler's Youth and as their sons were briefly conscripted into the German army. Joseph Ratzinger's university studies were not just interrupted by the war, but his chief theological mentor was removed from his school by the Nazis. Ratzinger didn't just return to college after the war was over; he had to help literally rebuild the college because Allied bombs had partially destroyed it. [19]

The wars left Europe utterly changed. The disillusioning experience of inhuman violence meant that people didn't trust each other or institutions anymore. The prewar Germany that Joseph Ratzinger grew up in was a place where a profound respect for the Catholic faith was inculcated in him by the heartfelt expressions of faith in his school and parish and town. The postwar Germany that he entered as a priest and bishop was an aggressively secular place in which church attendance quickly became rare and the Church's voice unwelcome in the public square.

War always does that. At a general audience on September 14, 2014, Pope Francis described visiting the World War I memorial in Redipuglia, Italy. "There I prayed for those who fell in the Great War. The numbers are frightening: it is said that approximately eight million young soldiers fell and seven million civilians died. This tells us the extent to which war is madness! A madness from which mankind has not yet learned its lesson, because a second world war followed it." [20]

His conclusion: "Responding with war only increases evil and death!"

War is a tragedy even when the good guys win. At a general audience on July 14, 2013, Pope Francis recalled praying at the Cathedral of Lutsk for the seventieth anniversary of the Volhynia massacres, and noted how "the Second World War took a toll of tens of thousands of victims and wounded the brotherhood of two peoples, the Polish and the Ukrainian." [21]

Father Jorge, War Hero

Jorge Bergoglio's own Italian family lived in Argentina because, on the eve of World War II, they fled the fascism of Mussolini. While they had jobs in Argentina when they first arrived, the Bergoglios' heartache at leaving their homeland was soon exacerbated by the economic crisis that hit Argentina, along with the rest of the world, in 1932. The family had to scrape by, looking anywhere for work.

God brings good out of every evil, however. For Pope Francis, the bright spots are the heroes. He sees times of war as a call to heroism. When he visited New York City in 2015 he stopped at the Ground Zero memorial on September 25 and said, "This place of death became a place of life too, a place of saved lives, a hymn to the triumph of life over the prophets of destruction and death, to goodness over evil, to reconciliation and unity over hatred and division."[22]

It should be noted that Pope Francis was himself a hero of unity and reconciliation in a time of war. Journalist Nello Scavo tells the story in his book *Bergoglio's List*, which was first published in Italian in 2013, and in English translation in 2015. The title compares the career of Oskar Schindler in World War II with Father Jorge Mario Bergoglio's actions as a Jesuit superior in Argentina during the "Dirty War."

Scavo describes how, shortly after Pope Francis's election, he began to research the new pope's relationship with the Dirty War in Argentina. "As my journalistic investigation progressed, from time to time, I began to hear about dissidents who had been protected and saved by the future pope during those terrible years."[23]

He decided to look further into the matter, and the result is a body of research and interviews that shows that Father Jorge "risked his life to save approximately 100 people who had been identified as 'enemies' of the Argentinian junta." The priest saved dozens more by warning them before the authorities could catch them.

The Dirty War started in 1976 when military generals launched a coup d'etat that ousted President Isabel Martínez de Perón, the third wife of longtime popular ruler Juan Perón, who had died in 1974. The armed forces who took control were brutal. They toppled the government, abolished the constitution, and dissolved the Congress and Supreme Court. They outlawed political dissent, banned labor unions, and seized control of newspapers and news agencies.

"The viciousness of the junta's campaign against its opponents is difficult to comprehend," Scavo writes. "The junta created a 'climate of terror' in which political opponents were jailed and tortured, forced to give up the names of others. Then, the prisoners often 'disappeared,' a euphemism for any number of cruel ends: shot dead or dropped into the ocean from helicopters."[24]

Father Bergoglio, superior of the Jesuits in Argentina, began helping rescue targets of the coup, regardless of their beliefs. Scavo tells the story of Gonzalo Mosca, an anticlerical left-wing labor organizer who was hiding out in the suburbs of Buenos Aires. His brother contacted Father Jorge, who picked up Mosca in his car and brought him to the Jesuit College of San Miguel. The priest hid him there for four days while he organized an escape plan that included travel by air and boat to a Brazilian Jesuit house and then a transcontinental flight to Europe.

Mosca told Scavo, "I don't know of other people who would have done the same thing. I don't know if anyone else would have saved me without knowing me at all."[25]

And so it is that Pope Francis takes a dim view of war.

As to the accusation that war is sometimes necessary and that the papal vision of a loving brotherhood of man is an unhelpful distraction, one need only look at Poland. There you have an example of what happens when a dynamic Christian leader—Karol Wojtyla, who would later become Pope John Paul II—faces down oppressors by spreading hope and teaching the dignity of man. As Yale historian John Gaddis put it:

> When John Paul II kissed the ground at the Warsaw airport on June 2, 1979, he began the process by which communism in Poland—and ultimately everywhere else in Europe—would come to an end.... "The pope!" Joseph Stalin was reputedly fond of asking. "How many divisions has he got?" John Paul II, during the nine days he spent in in Poland in 1979, provided the answer.[26]

When he was tending the roots of the solidarity movement as a Polish bishop, Pope John Paul II lived as part of an oppressed dissenting organization in a Soviet country. At the end of Pope John Paul's life, Poland's Catholic faith was a force to be reckoned with worldwide. Catholics in many American cities are familiar with the phenomenon of Polish priests serving American parishes. Catholics in Great Britain's cities increasingly see Polish parishes being served by Great Britain's church. "Devout Poles show Britain how to keep the faith,"[27] said the *Guardian* newspaper in 2006, noting that Mass attendance and confession were way up in the country because of Polish immigrants.

Without violence, Pope John Paul II did what no war in the twentieth century could do: He brought about not just peace but a renaissance of faith and the human spirit. But you needn't be a history-making pope or a rescue hero to help promote peace, Pope Francis said at the National September 11 Memorial (Ground Zero) in Manhattan. We can all play a part in making a new civilization of peace and justice a reality. "This can only happen if we uproot from our hearts all feelings of hatred, vengeance and resentment," he said. "We know that that is only possible as a gift from heaven."[28]

He asked each person present to spend a moment offering themselves to God as an agent of peace in the world: "Peace in our homes, our families, our schools and our communities. Peace in all those places where war never seems to end. Peace for those faces which have known nothing but pain. Peace throughout this world which God has given us as the home of all and a home for all."[29]

Referring to the heroes of 9/11 Pope Francis said, "The lives of our dear ones will not be lives which will one day be forgotten. Instead, they will be present whenever we strive to be prophets not of tearing down but of building up, prophets of reconciliation, prophets of peace."[30]

CHAPTER FIVE

Welcoming the Unborn

"The moment the sound of your greeting reached my ears,
the infant in my womb leaped for joy."
—Luke 1:44

"Hello, Anna, this is Pope Francis."

Those are the words Anna Romano heard when she picked up the phone on September 3, 2013. She later told an Italian newspaper about it, and the story helped give fans a new reason to love Francis—and a new nickname, "the cold-call pope."

Instead of going through intermediaries to contact the few important people a pope has to consult, Pope Francis throughout his pontificate has taken to simply picking up the phone and calling people himself—and not just important advisers.

The pope explained his reasons to Vatican Television director Msgr. Dario Viganò according to the Catholic magazine *Famiglia Cristiana*. "Tell the journalists that my calls are not news," Pope Francis told him. "I've always done this, even in Buenos Aires."

When the pope wanted to reach out to someone who sent a card or letter, he told Viganò, "For me, it's much easier to call, to ask about the problem and suggest a solution, if there is one. Some people I call, others I write to instead."[1]

In August he reached out by phone to comfort a woman who had been raped by a police officer in Argentina. He also called Michele Ferri, an Italian man who had suffered a "series of tragedies in the family" including his brother's murder in a gas station robbery.

"Hello, Michele, it's Pope Francis," he said, and Ferri thought it was a joke, at first—he was only convinced when the pope mentioned the letter he had written. "I hadn't told anyone about it, not even my mother or my wife, and I knew that it was him," he said.[2]

After talking to the brother of the murder victim, Francis called their mother.

The calls can be a problem for Father Federico Lombardi, the pope's spokesman. Often, people have claimed that the pope called them and said things over the phone that imply a change in Catholic practices or papal permission to bend doctrinal rules. Lombardi has said his policy was to neither confirm nor deny the calls unless they touched on matters of "international relevance." When one such call arose, a young man in France saying the pope called to respond to his letter about homosexuality, Lombardi said, "I can deny with certainty that the pope has called a young man in France." Lombardi's worry is always that someone can call pretending to be the pope and cause confusion.

A Call for Life

But when thirty-five-year-old Anna Romano received a call from the pope, she said, "I recognized his voice and I knew right away that it really was the pope. I was petrified," she told Rome's *Il Messaggero* newspaper.[3]

Romano had written to the pope because her fiancé had urged her to abort their child when she discovered she was pregnant. She refused, and that led to another shock: The man was already married with a family of his own.

She told Francis how she felt "betrayed, humiliated." The pope spoke like "a dear, old friend," she said. He "reassured me, telling me that the baby was a gift from God, a sign of Providence. He told me I would not be left alone."

When Romano told the pope she worried about finding a pastor to baptize the baby, Pope Francis said he didn't think that would be a problem. "But if not," he added, "you know there's always me."[4]

If September started out as the month that Francis caused a stir as the "cold-call pope," it ended as the month where he was defined by a remarkable interview in *America* magazine by Jesuit Father Antonio Spadaro that came to define his papacy.

The day the interview was released, on September 19, 2013, headlines about the interview focused not on its majestic vision of the Church's missionary character or on the culture of encounter that Francis described, a culture exemplified by his cold calls—they focused on what it had to say about abortion and homosexuality.

First, Heal the Wounds

The New York Times, at first, headlined the story, "Pope Bluntly Faults Church's Focus on Gays and Abortion." Said *USA Today*: "Pope seeks less focus on abortion, gays, contraception." CBS News ran its version of the Associated Press report, calling it: "Pope Francis: Catholic Church Must Focus Beyond 'Small-Minded Rules.'"

There followed the same phenomenon that came after the "Who am I to judge?" comment. Some Catholics were convinced Pope Francis wanted to change the Church's teaching on abortion.

The day after those headlines hit, the pope had an opportunity to correct the misimpression. In a speech to Catholic healthcare professionals and gynecologists on September 20, 2013, he said: "Every child who, rather than being born, is condemned unjustly to being aborted, bears the face of Jesus Christ, bears the face of the Lord, who even before he was born, and then just after birth, experienced the world's rejection."[5]

Pope Francis was not remotely backing away from what the Church teaches about abortion. What he said in that interview is practically the opposite of that: He was not telling Catholics to ignore the hard teachings of the Church; he was telling Catholics to act on them more effectively.

"I see clearly," the pope said in his interview, "that the thing the Church needs most today is the ability to heal wounds and to warm the hearts of the faithful; it needs nearness, proximity. I see the church as a field hospital after battle. It is useless to ask a seriously injured person if he has high cholesterol and about the level of his blood sugars! You have to heal his wounds. Then we can talk about everything else. Heal the wounds, heal the wounds."[6]

But then he added, "The church sometimes has locked itself up in small things, in small-minded rules. The most important thing is the first proclamation: Jesus Christ has saved you."[7]

Pope Francis's remarks were in fact nothing new. An interviewer once asked Pope Benedict XVI why, when he was at the World Meeting of Families, even though he spoke twice, he didn't mention abortion, contraception, or homosexual marriage. Benedict answered: "I had only two opportunities to speak for 20 minutes. And when you have so little time you cannot immediately begin with 'no.' Firstly, you have to know what we really want, right? Christianity, Catholicism, is not a collection of prohibitions: it is a positive option. It is very important that we look at it again because this idea has almost completely disappeared today."[8]

But even if Pope Francis's advice was sound, wasn't his wording unfortunate? Why suggest that opposition to abortion is an "obsession" of the "small-minded"? Again, Pope Benedict XVI could be found guilty of the same charge. He once gave this advice to bishops:

> We should not allow our faith to be drained by too many discussions of multiple, minor details, but rather, should always keep our eyes in the first place on the greatness of Christianity. I remember, when I used go to Germany in the 1980s and '90s, that I was asked to give interviews and I always knew the questions in advance. They concerned the ordination of women, contraception, abortion and other such constantly recurring problems. If we let ourselves be drawn into these discussions, the Church is then identified with certain commandments or prohibitions; we give the impression that we are moralists with a few somewhat antiquated convictions, and not even a hint of the true greatness of the faith appears.[9]

Pope Francis put it this way: "We cannot insist only on issues related to abortion, gay marriage and the use of contraceptive methods," he said. "This is not possible. I have not spoken much about these things, and I was reprimanded for that. But when we speak about these issues, we have to talk about them in a context."[10]

We do not come to accept Jesus because Christian morality is challenging; we come to accept the challenge of Christian morality because we have fallen in love with Jesus. "The Church's pastoral ministry cannot be obsessed with the transmission of a disjointed multitude of doctrines to be imposed insistently," he said. "The proposal of the Gospel must be more simple, profound, radiant. It is from this proposition that the moral consequences then flow."[11]

Nor did Pope Francis mean that priests should go easy on the sin of abortion in the confessional. He meant that the Church should do both: Welcome sinners, and tell them the truth. Francis told Father Spadaro that the confessor "is always in danger of being either too much of a rigorist or too lax. Neither is merciful, because neither of them really takes responsibility for the person." A confessor should neither be a "rigorist" who doesn't address the real situation of the penitent, or a "loose minster" who says "This is not a sin."

This is the approach he models in his phone calls: He consoles the rape victim, comforts the family who suffers violence, and reaches out to the pregnant, unmarried woman.

THE WOMAN AT THE WELL

Jesus does the same thing in his meeting with the Samaritan woman at the well (see John 4:1–26). In their brief encounter, Jesus masterfully takes a woman who has led a sinful life from a simple conversation about water to a self-examination of her life, to a recognition that Jesus is the Messiah. He does it without ever voicing his clear objections to her sinful life.

The harder way, the respectful way, is the only way that works. This is what Francis is trying to do. Francis described the encounter by saying the Samaritan woman "encountered Jesus, spoke with him, and her life changed."[12] She has become a "witness to the Gospel…one who has encountered Jesus Christ, who knows him, or better, who feels known by him, recognized, respected, loved, forgiven." This imbues her with joy which is "passed on to others."

Jesus respects the woman's freedom, and so wins her over. In the Gospel account, Christ speaks in the woman's language about a real need the woman feels—in this case, for water. Too often, our efforts to tell other people about Christ fail to recognize their interests, while making our interests—that they give in to the power of our greater argument—very clear. Unless we evangelize as Jesus did at the well, we risk becoming "Christians who think of the faith as a system of ideas, as an ideology," he said. "Those who fall into casuistry or ideology are Christians who know doctrine but who lack faith. Like the demons, with the difference that the demons tremble, whereas these do not: They live in peace."[13]

Christ doesn't condemn the woman—rather, he leads her to a place where she can recognize who he is. Once she embraces him, she recalibrates her thinking. This is crucial. Not only do we frighten people away from us by being judgmental, we deny them the opportunity to find a way to truly repent. These are the two contrasting realities: on the one hand, there are "those who have doctrine and know things" and on the other there are "those who have faith…. Faith is an encounter with Jesus Christ, with God." The Samaritan woman achieves faith before mastering doctrine.

When Pope Francis faces the issue of abortion, he certainly believes what the Church believes. Abortion is the taking of a human life and under no circumstances can we kill one person to benefit another person. But he refuses to ignore the person who is most affected by the teaching on abortion: The pregnant woman in the terrible position of having to upend her life or end the unseen life inside her. Many such women never heard an honest person confront them with understanding about their predicament. They often discover too late that choosing abortion, not choosing birth, is what brings tragedy to their life.

"Abortion compounds the grief of many women who now carry with them deep physical and spiritual wounds after succumbing to the pressures of a secular culture which devalues God's gift of sexuality and the right to life of the unborn," Pope Francis told African bishops. Far from downplaying abortion, he said "we bishops and priests must give a consistent witness to the moral teaching of the Gospel…in season and out of season."[14]

That witness has to include both a witness to the truth of the matter and a witness to the Church's mercy. In his September 2015 letter Pope Francis announced a Jubilee Year of Mercy and wrote of women who have abortions, "I am well aware of the pressure that has led them to this decision. I know that it is an existential and moral ordeal. I have met so many women who bear in their heart the scar of this agonizing and painful decision." Whereas before priests needed a bishop's approval to absolve the sin of abortion, Francis said, "I have decided, notwithstanding anything to the contrary, to concede to all priests for the Jubilee Year the discretion to absolve of the sin of abortion those who have procured it and who, with contrite heart, seek forgiveness for it." Many dioceses in the world already allowed priests this privilege; Pope Francis wanted to make sure all did.[15]

So, in short, Pope Francis wanted the Church's teaching on abortion to put two people at its center: The mother and the child. In fact, this is precisely what the pro-life movement in the United States has been doing for years. The movement has reached out to women in many ways, from adoption services to clothing drives to postabortion counseling, when necessary. The approach has changed hearts and minds. In 2008, for the first time in years of polling on the question, more respondents told Gallup that they were pro-life than said they were pro-choice. Seven years later, however, pro-choice was on top again, and so the work continues.[16]

Part of the problem may be that abortion has become part of a partisan political profile, which blocks clear thinking about the issue. *Evangelii Gaudium* warned against two different political attitudes that obscure the abortion issue. On the one hand is the idea that it is possible to vote in ways that help keep abortion legal, so long as we are voting in opposition to other clear-cut issues such as war or the death penalty. On the other side is the attitude that a Catholic who votes for a pro-life candidate has fulfilled the full measure of a Christian's duty and need not trouble himself with other life issues or other pro-life action.

Pro-Life in the Public Square

Pope Francis's consistent witness to the teaching on the right to life has included standing up to politicians. As Archbishop of Buenos Aires, Jorge Bergoglio was the editor and architect of a pastoral plan for Latin American and Caribbean dioceses in 2007. The Aparecida Document, named for the shrine where bishops met to develop it, is strict on the subject of Catholic lawmakers who promote abortion. According to the document:

> We must adhere to "eucharistic coherence," that is, be conscious that they cannot receive holy communion and at the same time act with deeds or words against the commandments, particularly when abortion, euthanasia, and other grave crimes against life and family are encouraged. This responsibility weighs particularly over legislators, heads of governments, and health professionals.[17]

The document echoed a previous ruling by Cardinal Joseph Ratzinger. Shortly before becoming Pope Benedict XVI, as doctrinal head of the Church, Cardinal Ratzinger wrote a letter to Washington, DC, Cardinal Theodore McCarrick. When a politician promotes abortion with his or her political career, he wrote, "his Pastor should meet with him, instructing him about the Church's teaching, informing him that he is not to present himself for Holy Communion until he brings to an end the objective situation of sin, and warning him that he will otherwise be denied the Eucharist."[18]

In presenting the Latin American pastoral plan, Archbishop Bergoglio stressed its teaching on abortion, which he called "the death penalty for the unborn." He said, "the most mentioned word in the Aparecida Document is 'life' because the Church is very conscious of the fact that the cheapest thing in Latin America, the thing with the lowest price, is life." His outspoken views put him at loggerheads with Argentina's president Cristina Kirchner, who publicly challenged his insistence on life teachings.[19]

The same thing has happened in Rome in his relations with the city's mayor, Ignazio Marino. The pope made headlines by showing his irritation that the mayor had traveled to Cuba when he did. In an in-flight interview, reporters noted the anger with which Pope Francis told them in no uncertain terms that the mayor was not invited. "Pope calls Rome mayor a 'pretend Catholic' who supports gay marriage and euthanasia," said *Christianity Today* in a report about the Italian media's take on the incident.[20]

His ire at the architects of laws that undermine the right to life is rooted in his distinction between sin and corruption. Misdeeds from weak human beings who repent of the wrong they have done and try to do better is one thing; those who use their power to lock in sinful patterns that wound others is quite another. Francis sees the same potential for corruption in the tendency to feel satisfied with merely voting to oppose abortion while failing to engage on other life issues.

Calling unborn children among the "most defenseless and innocent among us" he writes in *Evangelii Gaudium*, "Frequently, as a way of ridiculing the Church's effort to defend their lives, attempts are made to present her position as ideological, obscurantist and conservative. Yet this defense of unborn life is closely linked to the defense of each and every other human right."[21]

Another hallmark of the pope's teaching on abortion is his tendency to put abortion into a list of other sins against the frail and the weak.

In a speech to Vatican diplomats his list of "frightful" atrocities against children included child soldiers and human trafficking.[22]

He clearly wants to show the world that Catholics are not obsessed about only a few issues but embrace them all. It is a fine line. He quickly reminded the ambassadors that "it is not 'progressive' to try to resolve problems by eliminating a human life." Similarly, in an interview with *La Voz del Pueblo* newspaper in Argentina, Pope Francis noted the irony of countries whose strict child-protection laws penalize parents for spanking their children, yet allow them to kill their children before they are born.[23]

Francis's political solution would be different. He spelled it out in a speech to the Rome-based Dignitatis Humanae Institute. He said lay Catholics, especially but not limited to those in politics, should be made more aware of the social teaching of the Church "so that they may think in accord with the Gospel and the social doctrine of the church" in order to protect "the unborn, the poorest, the sick and elderly, the seriously handicapped, etc."[24]

These are the people on the peripheries of society that Francis wants his "motherly Church" to reach out to. On October 4, 2013, he told the World Council of Churches that they should do the same. "We are called to reach out to those who find themselves in the existential peripheries," *he* said, "the most vulnerable of our brothers and sisters: the poor, the disabled, the unborn and the sick, migrants and refugees, the elderly and the young who lack employment."[25]

THE PASTOR

Pope Francis has shown in his own life exactly what he means. In his 2015 book *The Name of God Is Mercy*, Pope Francis tells the story of a single mother he knew as a parish priest in Argentina. "She did not have a steady job and only managed to find temporary jobs a couple months out of the year. When there was no work," he said, "she had to prostitute herself to provide her children with food."

She came to the church looking for help, and the parish provided what it could. One year at Christmastime, the woman returned and called for Father Jorge. "She had come to thank me," he said.

He thought she was thanking him for a package of food. "Yes, yes, thank you for that, too," she said. "But I came here today to thank you because you never stopped calling me Señora."

The experience taught Pope Francis to "welcome people delicately and not wound their dignity."[26]

This is how Pope Francis deals with women whose lives have been marked by the sin and tragedy of prostitution, abandonment, rape… and abortion.

On January 22, 2014, Pope Francis contacted via Twitter another group of people concerned with abortion. "I join the March for Life in Washington with my prayers," he announced. "May God help us respect all life, especially the most vulnerable."

CHAPTER SIX

Marriage, 2014–2015: Are Times a Changin'?

"For this reason a man shall leave his father and mother and be joined
to his wife, and the two shall become one flesh."
—Matthew 19:5

As 2013 changed to 2014, Pope Francis was the object of worldwide
adulation—which is not always a good thing.

Francis was the first pope to make the cover of *Rolling Stone*, over the
words "Pope Francis: The Times They Are a Changin.'" The accompanying article was strikingly uninformed.

"After the disastrous papacy of Benedict, a staunch traditionalist who
looked like he should be wearing a striped shirt with knife-fingered
gloves and menacing teenagers in their nightmares," wrote *Rolling
Stone's* Mark Binelli, "Francis' basic mastery of skills like smiling in
public seemed a small miracle to the average Catholic."[1] One doesn't
know where to begin to point out how wrong he was, both about the
humble and sweet-tempered Pope Benedict XVI who, yes, smiled regularly in public and about the new pope who shared Benedict's beliefs. in
fact, Francis actually tends to frown in his official appearances because
of chronic, painful health issues that make it difficult for him to be on
his feet for long stretches of time.

But the narrative in the *Rolling Stone* story matched in broad outline
the much better *Time* magazine article announcing that Pope Francis
would be "Person of the Year"—a title it took St. John Paul II fifteen
years in office to win. The *Times* article described the impact of the
Francis papacy this way:

> He is quoted saying of women who consider abortion because of
> poverty or rape, "Who can remain unmoved before such painful
> situations?" Of gay people: "If a homosexual person is of good

will and is in search of God, I am no one to judge." To divorced and remarried Catholics who are, by rule, forbidden from taking Communion, he says that this crucial rite "is not a prize for the perfect but a powerful medicine and nourishment for the weak."[2]

Managing editor Nancy Gibbs made sure the magazine didn't make the mistake of suggesting the pope was a radical departure from Benedict. In a nice turn of phrase, she wrote: "In less than a year, he has done something remarkable: He has not changed the words, but he's changed the music."[3]

But of the three issues that the magazine raised—abortion, homosexuality, and divorce—it was the third issue that would prove to be the biggest potential change for Pope Francis in the months to come.

RECEIVE "IN A WORTHY MANNER"?

There is a lot of misunderstanding about what the Church teaches about communion for Catholics who are divorced and remarried without an annulment. This happens for two simple reasons: We have forgotten the Church's teaching on Communion, and we have forgotten the Church's teaching on marriage.

The Church's teachings on the proper reception of the Eucharist have been largely forgotten, caught in the crosswinds of two conflicting realities within the twentieth-century Church: First, the faithful were encouraged to receive Communion more frequently; second, fewer were thoroughly catechized about when they should and should not receive Communion.

Historically, the Church stressed the majesty and unapproachability of the sacrament. The Church required yearly Communion precisely because so few received the sacrament regularly. In the twentieth century, the Church began to change that, first by lowering the Communion age to seven,[4] and second by promoting frequent Communion.[5]

By the time I received my First Communion in the 1970s, the pendulum had swung a long way away from "Catholics are overly cautious about communion" all the way to "Catholics are not much concerned about being ready to receive Communion." Because my family moved when I was young, I went through First Communion programs in two parishes. Neither one of them taught me about the real presence of Jesus Christ in the Eucharist, neither required first confession before First Communion, and neither mentioned that confession is sometimes required before receiving Communion. I only learned all of that in college—after receiving Communion without confession for a decade.

This is why bishops from the bishop of Rome on down have been so busy trying to explain the communion rule in the twenty-first century. So, a reminder: Catholics believe that in the Eucharist we partake of the actual Body and Blood of Christ.

Pope Francis explained how, in the sixth chapter of John, Jesus shocked the crowds by teaching this doctrine. Many "were scandalized because Jesus said: 'He who eats my flesh and drinks my blood has eternal life, and I will raise him up at the last day' (John 6:54). The listeners' astonishment is understandable.... What is meant by 'eat the flesh and drink the blood' of Jesus? Is it just an image, a figure of speech, a symbol, or does it indicate something real?" he asked. His answer:

> The Eucharist is Jesus himself who gives himself entirely to us. Nourishing ourselves of him and abiding in him through Eucharistic Communion, if we do so with faith, transforms our life, transforms it into a gift to God and to our brothers and sisters. Nourishing ourselves of that "Bread of Life" means entering into harmony with the heart of Christ, assimilating his choices, his thoughts, his behavior.[6]

This makes the Eucharist ground zero of the transformation in Christ that the Church calls us to. But it also means that Communion and confession are inextricably linked—and have been since the beginning. St. Paul put it this way: "Therefore whoever eats the bread or drinks the cup of the Lord unworthily will have to answer for the body and blood of the Lord. A person should examine himself, and so eat the bread and drink the cup" (1 Corinthians 11:27–28).

Church teaching distinguishes two kinds of sins. As St. John put it, "If anyone sees his brother sinning, if the sin is not deadly, he should pray to God and he will give him life.... All wrongdoing is sin, but there is sin that is not deadly" (1 John 5:16–17).

The Church calls the two types of sin *mortal* (that is, deadly) sin and *venial* sin. St. John Paul II often reminded Catholics that only those who have received absolution in the sacrament of reconciliation after committing a mortal sin can receive Communion. The most notable instance of this was in his encyclical on the Eucharist:

> The *Catechism of the Catholic Church* rightly stipulates that "anyone conscious of a grave sin must receive the sacrament of Reconciliation before coming to communion." I therefore desire to reaffirm that in the Church there remains in force, now and in the future, the rule by which the Council of Trent gave concrete expression to the Apostle Paul's stern warning when it affirmed that, in order to receive the Eucharist in a worthy manner, "one must first confess one's sins, when one is aware of mortal sin."[7]

The Aparecida Document, the 2007 pastoral plan from Latin America directed in large part by the future Pope Francis, puts the rule this way: "We live in a culture marked by strong relativism and a loss of the sense of sin which leads us to forget the need for the sacrament of Reconciliation in order to worthily approach receiving the Eucharist."[8]

The Eucharist is the real presence of the Second Person of the Trinity—the body, blood, soul, and divinity of Jesus Christ. As the US bishops point out in their 2006 document, "Happy Are Those Who Are Called to His Supper: On Preparing to Receive Christ Worthily in the Eucharist," there are many people excluded from receiving the Eucharist. Communion is only open to those Catholics who:

— Have gone to confession in the past year, or after a serious sin (the bishops even include examples: missing Mass on any Sunday or holy day of obligation, participating in abortion, viewing pornography, any extra-marital sex, etc.).

— Have fasted, "refraining from food and drink (except for water and medicines) for at least one hour prior to receiving Holy Communion."

— Are wearing "modest and tasteful dress...clothes that reflect our reverence for God and that manifest our respect for the dignity of the liturgy and for one another."

— Are in a recollected and prayerful state of mind.[9]

Why is communion so restrictive? Pope Francis often mentions the sacraments of penance and the Eucharist together as complementary sacraments that together mold us into a new person. He told young visitors to the Vatican in June 2013, Jesus "really gives his Body for us and pours out his Blood to redeem humanity's sins and to bring us into communion with him. In Penance, Jesus accepts us with all our limitations, he brings us the mercy of the Father who forgives us and transforms our heart, making it a new heart that can love as he does."

Many Catholics have never heard of this basic Eucharistic practice, and yet many people *have* heard that Catholics who are divorced and remarried without receiving an annulment cannot receive Communion. It understandably makes them angry to think that the Church gives Communion to anyone and everyone but singles out those who are in a second marriage.

But even for those who do know that Communion is restrictive, it can still feel harsh and unwarranted to withhold Communion from couples based on their marital status. And that brings us to the second misunderstanding: Our misunderstanding about marriage. While Catholics were forgetting how real Communion is, we were also forgetting how real marriage is.

THE MEANING OF MARRIAGE

As Pope Francis points out in his apostolic exhortation *Amoris Laetitia*, the language of the Bible is very suggestive when it speaks about the creation of man and woman. Says Genesis: "Then God said: Let *us* make human beings in *our* image, after our likeness." Then, a little later on, the text says, "God created mankind in his image; in the image of God he created *them*; male and female he created them. God blessed them and God said to them: Be fertile and multiply" (Genesis 1:26–28, emphasis added).

In this first account in Genesis, men and women aren't created separate from each other—we are created as one. You can see the unity of man and woman already. We are made, together, in his image. We are both needed to complete each other.

There is another account of the creation of man and woman in Genesis. In the second account, the story is told a little differently. God makes Adam first, and says, "It is not good for the man to be alone. I will make a helper suited to him" (Genesis 2:18). God puts Adam into a deep sleep and in a sense recreates him, taking Eve from his side. The original language intends us to understand that Eve came from the "guts" or "heart" of him—from his very center, leaving a kind of void.

This is so much the case that Adam, when he first sees Eve, has a moment of self-revelation. When he sees Eve, he also sees who he really is for the first time. "This one, at last, is bone of my bones and flesh of my flesh" (Genesis 2:23). Pope Francis says in *Amoris Laetitia*, "The original Hebrew suggests a direct encounter, face to face, eye to eye, in a kind of silent dialogue, for where love is concerned, silence is always more eloquent than words."[10] Isn't that very much the experience a couple has when they fall in love? They discover their true selves in their love for the other.

The *Catechism* makes this self-revelation even greater, teaching that the couple discovers their relationship with God in their love for each other. "The Holy Spirit is the seal of the marriage covenant, the ever available source of their love and the strength to renew their fidelity" (*CCC* 1644). In other words, the Holy Spirit, who is the seal of the love of the Father and Son, is the seal of the love of husband and wife.

The *Catechism* spells out how total their union is: Conjugal love "aims at a deeply personal unity, a unity that, beyond union in one flesh, leads to forming one heart and soul" (*CCC* 1643). One heart and one soul. Not just feelings of romantic unity, but real unity that doesn't depend on feelings. Unity that wouldn't think of any infidelity. Unity without barriers, unity open to all the surprises life has to throw at it. Unity that doesn't end—that is indissoluble.

Pope Francis says the Church's understanding of marriage is simply the same understanding that lovers have. "Lovers do not see their relationship as merely temporary. Those who marry do not expect their excitement to fade. Those who witness the celebration of a loving union, however fragile, trust that it will pass the test of time," he said. "The lasting union expressed by the marriage vows is more than a formality or a traditional formula; it is rooted in the natural inclinations of the human person."[11]

It is also the understanding God has, he said, quoting God's words through the prophet Malachi: "Let none be faithless to the wife of his youth. For I hate divorce, says the Lord" (Malachi 2:14–16). And quoting the Jesuit saint Robert Bellarmine: "The fact that one man unites with one woman in an indissoluble bond, and that they remain inseparable despite every kind of difficulty, even when there is no longer hope for children, can only be the sign of a great mystery."[12]

Given all the Church teaches about marriage, the rift of divorce is therefore not just the parting of a couple, or a change of plans, but the breaking of a bond that is established in Jesus Christ and held together by the Holy Spirit. It is also often the splitting of children from their home with a mother and father.

How is this different from an annulment? In an annulment, a couple, with the Church, determines that there was no sacramental bond in the first place. In order to enter into this holy bond, both partners must be able to freely and fully consent to enter into its essential dimensions: They must recognize the indissoluble nature of marriage, they must intend to be faithful to their spouse, and they must be open to life, willing to welcome children through their union.

If the drop-off in catechesis in the late twentieth century left many people without rudimentary knowledge of the Eucharist, it also left many people without this understanding of marriage. Many people have gotten married in the Catholic Church without realizing what it means: Marriage is a promise you can't take back. Many got married without being open to life. Consequently, many entered marriages that were later annulled, a point Pope Francis made to great controversy in June 2016.

This understanding of the indissoluble nature of marriage didn't originate with the Church—it came from Jesus Christ himself when he said, "Whoever divorces his wife and marries another commits adultery against her; and if she divorces her husband and marries another, she commits adultery" (Mark 10:11–12). It must be admitted that this Gospel passage has caused much heartache over the years—from King Henry VIII's decision to break from the Catholic Church to our friends or family members who have experienced the pain of being unable to receive communion after being divorced and remarried without an annulment. The Church's canon law provides options for those who need to separate from their spouses in cases that are truly intolerable.

Pope Francis addressed these situations in *Amoris Laetitia*.

> In some cases, respect for one's own dignity and the good of the children requires not giving in to excessive demands or preventing a grave injustice, violence or chronic ill-treatment. In such cases, separation becomes inevitable. At times it even becomes morally necessary, precisely when it is a matter of removing the more vulnerable spouse or young children from serious injury due to

abuse and violence, from humiliation and exploitation, and from disregard and indifference.

He added that even in these cases, "separation must be considered as a last resort, after all other reasonable attempts at reconciliation have proved vain."[13]

What Pope Francis is doing by raising this issue of communion for remarried Catholics is to assure those who wish to be reconciled with the Church that all is not lost because of tragic mistakes or unfortunate circumstances in the past. On his flight from America back to Rome, the pope told reporters that the Church's streamlined annulment procedures are not meant to be more lax on marriage but to be more merciful. "Those who think this is equivalent with 'Catholic divorce' are mistaken," he told reporters. "Marriage is indissoluble when it is a sacrament. And this the Church cannot change. It is doctrine. It is an indissoluble sacrament."[14]

Rather, he said, new annulment procedures are meant to determine whether "what seemed to be a sacrament wasn't a sacrament, for lack of freedom, for example, or for lack of maturity, or for mental illness, or there are so many reasons…that there was no sacrament." He gave examples when an annulment might be in order, recalling how, in Buenos Aires, he often saw women getting married because they were pregnant. "We called them 'speedy weddings.' They were to keep up appearances. Then babies are born; and some work out, but there's no freedom. Others go wrong little by little; they separate and say: 'I was forced to get married because we had to cover up this situation.'" He summed up the point by saying, "'Catholic divorce' does not exist. Nullity is granted if the union never existed, but if it did, it is indissoluble."

Even in that circumstance, all is not lost, he added on his flight back from the Holy Land in May 2014. "Something Pope Benedict said three times about the divorced has helped me a lot," he said. "The divorced are not excommunicated, and so many times they are treated as excommunicated."[15] He is right: Not being able to receive Communion is very different from excommunication. Many people are unable to receive Communion but remain full members of the Catholic Church.

Pop Francis writes about this painful circumstance in the interview-based book *The Name of God Is Mercy* when he describes the experience of a Catholic he knows well who was in a second marriage that prevented him from receiving the sacraments.

"I have a niece who was married to a man in a civil wedding before he received the annulment of his previous marriage," said the pope. "They wanted to get married, they loved each other, they wanted children, and they had three. The judge had even awarded him custody of the children from his first marriage. This man was so religious that every Sunday, when he went to Mass, he went to the confessional and said to the priest, 'I know you can't absolve me but I have sinned by doing this and that, please give me a blessing.' This is a religiously mature man."[16]

But while it is absolutely true that the indissolubility of marriage is hard for many couples—for far, far more people, it has been an enormous blessing. Pope Francis stressed this in his visit to America. Putting aside his prepared text at the Benjamin Franklin Parkway, he gave impromptu remarks on the family.

"Families have difficulties. Families—we quarrel; sometimes plates can fly; and children bring headaches. I won't speak about mothers-in-law," he smiled. "However, in families, there is always light because of the love of God's Son. Just as there are problems in families, there is the light of the Resurrection," he said. "The family is a factory of hope."[17]

And it is true: Studies show this resurrection effect. Married relationships typically have cycles of joy and difficulty. Couples are deeply satisfied with their marriages at times, and then they grow unsatisfied. Often, dissatisfied couples divorce. But those who stay together are soon reporting satisfaction again—often at a higher, more consistent level.

Those who start a new marriage are soon reporting dissatisfactions again in the same cycle in a new relationship.

Many married couples feel blessed by the Church's teaching on marriage. It kept them together through the hard times and brought them far more happiness than they would have had without it. The Church's teaching isn't a harsh aberration. It is the simple understanding that young lovers have when they say, "I do." We believe that love is forever, that breaking up is an intolerable wound, that real love does not stop. The Church agrees: What we feel is true—and the commitment we make is real. But what if we are thinking "divorce is always an option"?

LOVE THAT IS FRUITFUL

In a meditation he gave for couples on June 2, 2014, Pope Francis spoke of how each spouse's commitment to the other mirrors Jesus Christ's love for the Church. Jesus's love has the same three features as spousal love, he said: It is faithful, it perseveres and it is open to life—fruitful.

"Jesus is the faithful one," he said, the one who forgives and returns again and again when we offend him. "There are hard times. Many times you argue. But in the end you return, you ask for forgiveness and the matrimonial love goes forward, like the love of Jesus for the Church." The true measure of love is how well it perseveres. The greatest lovers are "the man and woman who get up every morning and bring their family forward."[18]

But he was at his most colorful in talking about the fruitfulness of marriage. "Jesus does not like marriages in which couples do not want children, in which they want to remain fruitless," he said. He called such situations a product of "the well-off culture of ten years ago." Couples began saying, "Not having children is better. That way you can travel and see the world, you can have a house in the country and relax!" In this vision of marriage, "it is more comfortable to have a little dog and two cats. Love is given to the two cats and the little dog."

He was quick to add that "sometimes the Lord does not send children" as a special cross whereby "Jesus makes his bride fruitful, renders the Church fruitful with new children and baptisms." But Christian love does not choose fruitlessness on its own. For deliberately fruitless marriages, "old age arrives in solitude, with the bitterness of awful loneliness."

The roller coaster life of joys and sorrows, crosses and resurrections that come with fidelity, perseverance, and openness to life turns out to be the greatest fulfillment an individual can have. Starting a family is the quickest way to enter the kind of self-giving, sacrificial love by which Christ built the Church. When I, the sinner, live just for myself, I am led to idolatry and selfishness. When I, the sinner, exist for others, I walk in Jesus's footsteps. Yet, Pope Francis often notes, Europe's birthrate is far below even replacement level.

As he told couples in a Valentine's Day meeting, a good marriage is the work of a fine craftsman. As tools, couples have the most important words in a marriage: "Please?" "May I?" and "I'm sorry." He said ultimately, married couples should live such that people will look at the wife and say: "Look at that beautiful woman, so strong! With the husband that she has, it's understandable!" They will look at the husband and say: "Look at him and the presence he has! With the wife he has, I can understand why!"[19]

Marriage Making Headlines

In October 2013, Pope Francis announced that the following year would be an Extraordinary General Assembly of the Synod of Bishops on the Family (hereafter, Synod on the Family). Not long after this, divorce and remarriage and communion rules began to dominate headlines about Pope Francis.

First, in November of 2013, the Vatican released a preparatory document for the upcoming synod. That first document raised the issue of communion for the divorced and remarried. "What questions do divorced and remarried people pose to the Church concerning the Sacraments of the Eucharist and of Reconciliation?" it asked, significantly. "Among those persons who find themselves in these situations, how many ask for these sacraments?"

Then, at a February 2014 meeting preparing for the Synod on the Family, German Cardinal Walter Kasper gave an in-depth argument for a "smaller segment of the divorced and remarried" to be admitted, as in Orthodox Churches, to "the sacrament of penance and then of Communion."[20] He had been making the proposal as early as 1993 as bishop of Rottenburg-Stuttgart in 1993, according to the *National Catholic Reporter*.[21] Pope John Paul II rejected the proposal but made Kasper a cardinal in 2001.

Shortly after his own election, Pope Benedict XVI promoted Cardinal Kasper, confirming him as president of the Pontifical Council for Promoting Christian Unity. Pope Francis followed in his predecessors' footsteps, entrusting responsibilities to the cardinal with full knowledge of his marriage views, appointing him to the Synod on the Family meetings in 2014 and 2015.

Soon, though, five cardinals, including American Cardinal Raymond Burke and the Vatican's faith watchdog, Cardinal Gerhard Müller, responded to Cardinal Kasper's proposal in their 2014 book *Remaining in the Truth of Christ: Marriage and Communion in the Catholic Church*. They argued that the Church's teaching on this matter is rooted in Christ's words in the Gospel and is not subject to change. Cardinals at loggerheads with each other are sure to be covered breathlessly as being in an epic battle—and that is what happened in the matter of the Kasper communion proposal.

In June 2014, the Vatican released a second document to set the stage for the Synod on the Family, to be held the following October. It didn't envision the Church changing doctrine; it envisioned the Church finding a better way to give spiritual support to couples who cannot receive communion:

A more painful wound results when these people remarry and enter a state of life which does not allow them to receive Holy Communion. Clearly, in these cases, the Church must not assume an attitude of a judge who condemns, but that of a mother who always receives her children and nurses their wounds so they may heal. With great mercy, the Church is called to find forms of "accompaniment" which can support her children on the path of reconciliation.[22]

Another wrinkle in the story came with the long-expected November 8 announcement that Cardinal Raymond Burke, a major opponent of Cardinal Kasper's proposal, would move from his Vatican post as prefect of the Apostolic Signatura—the "Supreme Justice" of the Vatican high court—to become patron of the Order of Malta. "Pope Francis Demotes Outspoken American Cardinal," said the Reuters story, repeating the understanding of the move as payback for his traditional marriage beliefs. Catholics who appreciated Cardinal Burke's candor on hot-button issues worried that Pope Francis was showing his hand—and using the back of it against adversaries.

In fact, Cardinal Burke's was the longest term a cardinal has had as prefect of the Apostolic Signatura in thirty-seven years. And as several Vatican watchers pointed out, if Pope Francis was trying to fire outspoken people, how did he miss Cardinal George Pell? And if he wanted to silence Cardinal Burke, why put him in a position where he was freer to be outspoken? One factor was the cardinal's view on annulment reform versus the synod's. And Pope Francis later explained in an interview with *La Nacion* that he had made the Malta decision with Cardinal Burke's approval, well before the synod, but kept Cardinal Burke in his old position longer than he otherwise would have so that he could be involved in the synod.[23]

THE APARECIDA DOCUMENT

At any rate, despite the stories about intrigue and behind-the-scenes machinations, Pope Francis wasn't trying to rig the synod to change

Church teaching—he was trying to open the synod to the fresh air of the Holy Spirit, in much the way he did for the meeting of Latin American bishops that produced the Aparecida Document. What he had done at Aparecida was a revelation to the Church and the document it produced was a "Light from the South" according to a June 13, 2012, *First Things* article by George Weigel. "This master plan for the New Evangelization in Latin America is…an entirely admirable piece of work that should be known throughout the world Church," said Weigel.

He noted aspects of the pastoral plan that will sound very familiar to those who have studied Pope Francis. According to the document, said Weigel, every Catholic "is baptized to be a 'missionary disciple.'" Everywhere is mission territory, and everything in the Church must be mission-driven." The document, he said, centers everything on the person of Jesus Christ, insisting that "the whole purpose of evangelism is to foster friendship with Jesus Christ, the Son of God."[24]

Weigel interviewed Cardinal Bergoglio, and the future pope cited three things that brought success to the document: the nearness of Our Lady, the contact the bishops had with ordinary laypeople who were visiting the shrine, and lots of prayer. Weigel summed up the interview this way: "The Aparecida experience suggests that good things happen at mass meetings of bishops when the bishops live like pastors, in close contact with their people, and when their deliberations seem more like the Upper Room of the Acts of the Apostles than an annual stockholders' meeting. The Aparecida Document also suggests that Latin America is far more than just the demographic center of the Catholic Church."

When biographer Austen Ivereigh looked back at those meetings from the hindsight of one who knew that a future pope was forged there, he saw the Aparecida gathering as an explanation of what Pope Francis's synod process would look like.

> The Aparecida gathering offered a glimpse of what the synod of bishops in Rome could be. Rather than working from a

predetermined document, it began with a diagnosis of contemporary culture and trends from each country, then worked them into concrete issues that could be discussed. It was bottom-up, not, as in the synods, top-down. Key to its success were warm relationships between the different national bishops' conferences, and a close friendship between the two principals, the CELAM president, Cardinal Errázuriz, and the chair of the drafting committee, Cardinal Bergoglio.[25]

The Aparecida Document was a revelation to the Latin American Church and to the Church in whole. It rejected the stage-managed style that prevailed in Church meetings and aimed for a process of input and feedback coming from many directions. And it worked—largely because the future Pope Francis stood in the center, directing traffic.

When it came time to gather a synod of bishops at the Vatican to discuss family policy, he took the same approach: A looser, more collegial, Aparecida-style synod. In October 2014 in Rome, the result was very different from Aparecida's triumph. The transparency of the synod was entirely new to the media, unaccustomed to watching bishops' meetings in progress. As a result, the media reported draft language and half-formed new ideas and caused a lot of confusion.

As he did at Aparecida, Pope Francis himself spelled out the results of the conference in a 2016 postsynod apostolic exhortation called *Amoris Laetitia* (The Joy of Love). The document is a full-throated defense of Church doctrines regarding marriage, but also a whole-hearted attempt to find ways to welcome couples in irregular situations.

"The indissolubility of marriage—'what God has joined together, let no man put asunder' [Matthew 19:6]—should not be viewed as a 'yoke' imposed on humanity, but as a 'gift' granted to those who are joined in marriage" he writes, quoting the Synod fathers.[26]

But how to guard that principle in today's world? Pope Francis said, "There are two ways of thinking which recur throughout the Church's history: casting off and reinstating. The Church's way, from the time of the Council of Jerusalem, has always been the way of Jesus, the way of mercy and reinstatement.... The way of the Church is not to condemn anyone forever."[27]

There are many precedents for this approach. Take slavery for instance. The Church has never condoned chattel slavery, but from serfdom to military service, indentured servitude to live-in domestic help, the Church has had to discern what economic arrangements short of chattel slavery are acceptable. The question of whether and which slaveholders should be denied communion has been complicated and has varied from location to location.

In *Amoris Laetitia*, Pope Francis lists changes in circumstances that have undermined marriage in our time worldwide, including polygamy, forced marriages, and the widespread practice of cohabitation. He sums up the problem at the root of all of these misunderstandings about marriage as individualism: "Many countries are witnessing a legal deconstruction of the family, tending to adopt models based almost exclusively on the autonomy of the individual will," he writes. As a result, "In various countries, legislation facilitates a growing variety of alternatives to marriage, with the result that marriage, with its characteristics of exclusivity, indissolubility and openness to life, comes to appear as an old-fashioned and outdated option."[28]

This in turn means that many people, including many Catholics, have entered marriages with a worldly instead of sacramental understanding of marriage, never consciously intending to make the promises that Church teaching holds them to. And given the current state of marriage, Francis said, the Church must avoid "pigeonholing" or "classifying" all divorced and remarried people. The Synod, he said, called it a pastor's job to "adequately distinguish" between circumstances and "carefully discern situations," and he added, "We know that no 'easy recipes' exist."[29]

Father Dwight Longenecker in a column gave a priest's perspective of the approach Pope Francis is suggesting. To avoid invading anyone's privacy, he created composite couples from real situations he has encountered.[30]

First, Father Longenecker presented Bob, a "child of the 1960s" whose "first marriage was at the beach to a fellow love child when she got pregnant when they were both high." That marriage didn't last even a year, and Bob married twice more. The third wife was a lapsed Catholic who rediscovered her faith after the wedding. Bob, too, became convinced of the faith and wanted to enter the Church but could not track down his first wife to see if she would participate in an annulment. Should these two be denied the sacraments of confession and Communion?

Next, we meet Lucy, married for twenty-five years to Phil. "They were both Catholics and they got married in church after proper preparation," wrote Father Longenecker. But then, Phil left Lucy for a male lover, declaring that he had always been gay. The two divorced, and then Lucy got more involved in her local Catholic church. There she met Harold, whose first wife passed away. She wanted to annul her marriage to Phil, feeling it was probably not valid anyway, but Phil was not willing to help. She married Harold anyway. Should the two remain barred from confession and Communion?

These situations—and even more difficult situations in Third World countries—are what Pope Francis has in mind. "A pastor cannot feel that it is enough simply to apply moral laws to those living in 'irregular' situations, as if they were stones to throw at people's lives," wrote Francis. "This would bespeak the closed heart of one used to hiding behind the Church's teachings, 'sitting on the chair of Moses and judging at times with superiority and superficiality difficult cases and wounded families.'"

Instead, he called for pastors to wade into the difficulty of each situation and try to determine how the Church's principles apply. "The Church possesses a solid body of reflection concerning mitigating factors and situations. Hence it can no longer simply be said that all those in any 'irregular' situation are living in a state of mortal sin and are deprived of sanctifying grace."[31]

Among those mitigating circumstances, he says, the *Catechism* cites "ignorance, inadvertence, duress, fear, habit, inordinate attachments, and other psychological or social factors" (*CCC* 1735).

The fact is that many people in irregular marital situations today often simply find another faith to practice. Pope Francis is painfully aware of this. In his book *The Great Reformer*, Austen Ivereigh tells the story of Anglican Bishop Tony Palmer, whom Pope Francis met shortly after Palmer's ordination as an Anglican priest. Tony and his wife, Emiliana, had been introduced to sacramental Christianity through the Charismatic movement. Emiliana returned to her Catholic faith while Tony pursued Anglicanism.

When Cardinal Bergoglio asked Palmer about the ecumenical marriage, Palmer told him everything that was going well. Then, "I told him since I led my family back to the Catholic Church I am not allowed to take Communion. I have to stay in the benches on Sunday morning. So my kids come back after taking Communion and say, 'Dad, why would you join us to a church that separates a family?'" Palmer said that when the cardinal heard that his "heart broke—his eyes filled with tears." [32]

And so it is that *Rolling Stone* was wrong and *Time* magazine was right. The times are *not* a-changing, at least as regards marriage in the Catholic Church under Pope Francis. But we clearly have a pope who is eager to expand access to the sacraments.

CHAPTER SEVEN

Unity in the Church of Martyrs and Refugees

"Father, keep them in your name that you have given me, so that they
may be one just as we are."
—John 17:11

On January 3, 2014, in the middle of the night, masked gunmen began
knocking on doors in the Libyan coastal town of Sirte. They dragged
men out of bed and looked at their wrists. Every Christian they found
was dragged away at gunpoint.

Coptic Christians aren't hard to identify. Members of the ancient
Egyptian Church wear tattooed crosses on their wrists—a bold statement about their Christian identity, but also a safety measure. It allows
churches to stop non-Copts from entering services in an age of terrorism
and suicide bombings.[1]

The gunmen were Islamic State terrorists—ISIS—and the world
found out on February 15 why they were rounding up Christians. That
is the day a video appeared online, called "A Message Signed with Blood
to the Nation of the Cross." The brief video made with sophisticated
production values shows the men being led along a coastline by towering
masked figures dressed all in black, apparently made to look unnatu-
rally large through digital effects. The video depicts twenty-one fighters
forcing twenty-one prisoners dressed in orange to kneel in the sand.
Then the fighters behead their victims one by one on camera, warning
that they will attack Rome next.

Pope Francis was quick to call the slain Coptic men martyrs in
remarks the Monday after the video was released. "Today I read about
the execution of those twenty-one or twenty-two Coptic Christians," he
said. "Their only words were: 'Jesus, help me!' They were killed simply

because they were Christians. The blood of our Christian brothers and sisters is a witness that cries out to be heard. It makes no difference whether they be Catholics, Orthodox, Copts or Protestants. They are Christians! Their blood is one and the same. Their blood confesses Christ."[2]

Pope Francis saw the event as a call to ecumenism—the movement to reunite Christians: "I ask that we encourage one another to go forward with this ecumenism that is emboldening us, the ecumenism of blood," he said. "The martyrs belong to all Christians."

These Coptic Christian men do indeed make a powerful case for the unity of all Christians—and for a humane immigration policy. The men were migrant workers doing hard work in Libya to send money home to their impoverished families. Many of them came from the town of Al-Aour in Egypt. Reporters who collected their stories have provided us with an astonishing testament to what Christian life is like when it is fully lived.

Sophia Jones tells the story of Hani Abdel Messihah, thirty-two, who leaves behind four children—three girls and a boy—and a wife who remembered him as "gentle and kind," saying, "He took care of all of us. He gave us hugs and kisses…. He was an angel. There was a prayer in anything he said."

Yousef Shoukry was a twenty-four-year-old Coptic Christian who went to Libya for work despite the danger there. He said he wasn't afraid because God was with him. Shenouda Shoukry had high praise for his little brother: "He lived according to the book. I can't remember something he did wrong."[3]

The martyrs are described by their relatives as "very sweet," "easily embarrassed," "happiest being with [their] family and kids." You can hear in their stories the echoes of the first millennium of martyrs: "See how they loved each other."

They also show a powerful witness to the core beliefs and attitudes of Jesus Christ, who went to his own violent death forgiving his tormenters and promised eternal life to those who walked in his footsteps. Reporter Jonathan Rashad collected the impressions their families had of their martyrdoms.[4]

"We thank ISIS," said the mother of twenty-nine-year-old martyr Samuel Abraham. "Now more people believe in Christianity because of them. ISIS showed what Christianity is. We thank God that our relatives are in heaven. He chose them."

One young wife told him, "ISIS thought they would break our hearts. They did not. Milad is a hero now and an inspiration for the whole world."

Coptic Bishop Felobous, who is related to five of the martyrs, called for forgiveness. "Their leaving is painful. But we are not sad. We are proud of our martyrs. I congratulate ISIS. God is using them to bring martyrs to the world. Everything happens for a reason," he said, adding: "I was very sad when I heard the news of the air strikes led by the Egyptian military against ISIS. God asked us to love even our enemies."

Mathew Ayairga, the only black prisoner in the group, was not a Christian, according to one news agency's report, but he was forced to kneel on the beach with the others. He watched as the other prisoners confessed Christ and died for it. When it was Ayairga's turn, they asked him, "Do you reject Christ?" He answered, "Their God is my God," and so he was beheaded.[5]

Hana Aziz was one of the laborers who escaped the militants and hid in the desert. He told CNN reporters "To the last moment, the name of Jesus was on their lips. As they were being martyred, they were calling God's name, saying, 'God, have mercy on us.' The entire village is proud."[6]

Yes, and every Christian in the world—including every Catholic Christian—is proud that we have such brothers and sisters. We want to claim them for our own. But we can't, not totally. They would not receive communion in a Catholic church, nor would we in theirs. And not just Copts, of course. What is true of them is true of every Orthodox Christian Church and every Protestant denomination. The scandal of that lack of unity among people who share an "ecumenism of blood" is something that Pope Francis had been working to address since early in his pontificate.

THE ONE CHURCH

He shared another example of the "ecumenism of blood" on his flight from Istanbul to Rome. "When I was in Germany, I went to Hamburg to celebrate a baptism, and the parish priest was working on the cause for canonization of a priest who had been guillotined by the Nazis for having taught catechesis to the children," he said. "During his work on this cause, he discovered that in line behind the priest in question, there was a Lutheran pastor condemned to the guillotine for the same reason. The blood of these two mixed. And this parish priest went to the bishop and said: 'I'm not taking this cause forward only for the priest: It's either for both or for neither!'"[7]

Beheading is a suggestive metaphor in discussions of Christian unity. At a general audience, Pope Francis reminded Catholics that, according to St. Paul, the unity of the Church with Christ is the unity of a body with its head. "The Church is not a welfare, cultural or political association but a living body that walks and acts in history," he said. "And this body has a head, Jesus, who guides, feeds and supports it. This is a point that I would like to emphasize: if one separates the head from the rest of the body, the whole person cannot survive. It is like this in the Church: we must stay ever more deeply connected with Jesus."[8]

But Catholics further believe that there is a hierarchy within the body of Christ itself. This teaching, again, comes from Jesus Christ, who renamed the apostle Simon "Cephas," which means *rock* in Aramaic and is rendered "Petrus," or Peter, in Greek. "I say to you, you are Peter, and upon this rock I will build my church, and the gates of the netherworld shall not prevail against it. I will give you the keys to the kingdom of heaven. Whatever you bind on earth shall be bound in heaven; and whatever you loose on earth shall be loosed in heaven" (Matthew 16:18–19).

So to stay united does not just mean that each of us stays connected to Jesus in our own way, he said. We have to do it the way Jesus asked. "It means staying united to the pope and to the bishops who are instruments of unity and communion," he said. Then he lamented the many kinds of Christians that prevent the body from truly being one. "So much damage to the Church comes from division among Christians, from biases, from narrow interests. Division among us, but also division among communities: Evangelical Christians, Orthodox Christians, Catholic Christians, why are we divided? We must try to bring about unity. I will tell you something: today, before leaving home, I spent forty minutes, more or less, half an hour, with an evangelical pastor and we prayed together and sought unity."[9]

His intense desire for unity is very much like that of previous popes. "What unites us is much greater than what divides us," said St. John XXIII, who opened the Second Vatican Council. Pope John Paul II wrote an encyclical about the need for Christian unity, 1995's *Ut Unum Sint*. The title, "That They May Be One" comes from Jesus Christ's prayer for the Church on the night before he died: "I pray not only for them, but also for those who will believe in me through their word, so that they may all be one, as you, Father, are in me and I in you, that they also may be in us, that the world may believe that you sent me" (John 17:20–21).

St. John Paul II said that he longed so much for unity that he was willing to make changes to the way papal primacy is understood. "As Bishop of Rome," he wrote, "I am convinced that I have a particular responsibility…to find a way of exercising the primacy which, while in no way renouncing what is essential to its mission, is nonetheless open to a new situation."[10]

Pope Francis has the same willingness to change his own job description as far as he possibly can in order to regain Christian unity. He wrote to Pope Tawadros, the Alexandrian head of the Christian Copts, shortly after becoming pope, praising his openness to unity. After meeting with Russian Orthodox Bishop Hilarion in November 2013, he told reporters, "We have to continue in the footsteps of John Paul II [who said,] 'Help me to find a form of Primacy that we can agree on.'" He added that he discussed starting a process with the Russian Orthodox where they would do just that.[11]

It is important to keep in mind just what Church teaching says legitimate unity would look like in order to avoid a compromised unity that goes too far and gives up too much of what Jesus Christ asked of his Church when he told the Apostles the Holy Spirit would "guide [them] to all truth" (John 16:13). In the year 2000 Pope John Paul II and Cardinal Joseph Ratzinger promulgated the document *Dominus Iesus* (*The Lord Jesus*) which clearly lays out exactly where the Church does and does not see authentic unity.

"There exists a single Church of Christ, which subsists in the Catholic Church, governed by the Successor of Peter and by the Bishops in communion with him," it says. Then there are those Christians, such as the various Orthodox churches who "remain united to her by means of the closest bonds, that is, by apostolic succession and a valid Eucharist, are true particular Churches." These are fully Churches that can trace their history through the valid ordinations of priests and bishops all the way back to the Apostles and thus to Jesus Christ. They are separated from us mainly in that "they do not accept the Catholic doctrine of the Primacy, which, according to the will of God, the Bishop of Rome objectively has and exercises over the entire Church."

But then the document mentions Protestant denominations. These are not fully Churches, but "those who are baptized in these communities are, by Baptism, incorporated in Christ and thus are in a certain communion, albeit imperfect, with the Church." Next, *Dominus Iesus* adds something interesting: "Baptism in fact tends toward the full development of life in Christ through the integral profession of faith, the Eucharist, and full communion in the Church."[12] So, while these denominations don't have a connection to Christ through a historical succession of ordinations, they do have a real connection with him—and us—through baptism, and this cracks open the door to intercommunion.

INTERCOMMUNION

The question of intercommunion between Christians has been a subject of controversy for years, and Pope Francis has been criticized for being too permissive—too compromising—on the question. At a question and answer session on November 11, 2015, at a Lutheran church in Rome, a Lutheran woman asked him about intercommunion. "I ask myself: don't we have the same Baptism? If we have the same Baptism, shouldn't we be walking together?" said the pope. His impromptu remarks are hard to follow, but at one point he said, "I wouldn't ever dare to *allow* this, because it's not my competence. One baptism, one Lord, one faith. Talk to the Lord and then go forward. I don't dare to say anything more."[13]

His words do seem to want to open the door to intercommunion past what the Catholic Church allows. But coupled with his emphatic "I wouldn't ever dare to allow this," his words actually do work as a paraphrase of the *Catechism*, which says Protestant denominations "have not preserved the proper reality of the Eucharistic mystery in its fullness, especially because of the absence of the sacrament of Holy Orders. It is for this reason that, for the Catholic Church, Eucharistic intercommunion with these communities is not possible" (*CCC* 1400).

The real point of Pope Francis's words seems to be to emphasize the strong unity that our common baptism gives Catholics with Protestants. In fact, the Canon Law that regulates these matters, after directing that "Catholic ministers administer the sacraments licitly to Catholic members of the Christian faithful alone," spells out occasions when intercommunion with Orthodox Christians is allowable. Then it opens the door a crack for Protestants, too—"if the danger of death is present" or in some other "grave necessity." In those cases, the sacraments can be administered to a Protestant on an individual case-by-case basis if the person has no way to receive communion in their own denomination. In these cases, importantly, the person receiving Communion must "manifest Catholic faith in respect to these sacraments" and be "properly disposed." By that last qualifier Müller means that by allowing the sacraments, the Church is allowing for confession first and then Communion.[14]

This is truly only allowable on a rare, extreme, case-by-case basis. Canon Law instructs that bishops not issue general norms about the matter and not give Communion to groups of Protestants. This is why, when reports were issued that visiting priests tasked with distributing Communion—not the pope—had distributed Communion to Lutherans from Finland at St. Peter's Basilica, the Finland Catholic Information Center was quick to release a statement reminding reporters that intercommunion is still not possible.[15] However much we long for unity, the truth of the matter is that Christians are still not united, and to pretend that they are would add another wound to the already bruised conception of the truth.

In a relativistic age, when many suggest that truth is just a matter of opinion, insistence on the truth is a vital countersign. At a May 15, 2013, audience Pope Francis pointed to Christ as the answer to relativism. "We are living in an age in which people are rather skeptical of truth. Benedict XVI has frequently spoken of relativism, that is, of the tendency to consider nothing definitive and to think that truth comes from consensus or from something we like." He said the Church is the custodian of the truth because, "as Jesus promised, the Holy Spirit guides us 'into all the truth'; not only does he guide us to the encounter with Jesus, the fullness of the Truth, but he also guides us 'into' the Truth, that is, he makes us enter into an ever deeper communion with Jesus, giving us knowledge of all the things of God."[16]

Dominus Iesus traces the origins of today's widespread relativism to the time when the body of Christ was torn by divisions in the Great Schism in the Church and the many divisions of the Protestant Reformation.[17] Once people decided that they could all believe different things about the most important truth of them all—God—and accept each other's opposing doctrines as "true for them," it did not take long for people to believe that all truth was relative.

Notre Dame's Brad S. Gregory, in *The Unintended Reformation,* describes how the divisions of Christianity led first to violent disagreement about who was right and who was wrong, and then to an uneasy "agree to disagree" stalemate and finally to the presumption that *everyone* was right in their way. Because of the Reformation, "By the end of the twentieth century, increasing numbers of people, especially in Western Europe and Canada, had either made an atheistic inference that *no* religious claims are true, or drawn a skeptical conclusion that it cannot be known which among them might be.... Large numbers of religious believers, themselves influenced by these cultural currents and the desire to be inoffensive, in effect relativize and subjectivize their own truth claims, making clear they speak only for themselves."[18]

For Pope Francis, this is a problem that can only be solved by a united Christianity. Of course it has to be done properly. It doesn't make sense to try to heal the root cause of relativism by pretending that the different conceptions of the truth don't exist. But it seems to me that Pope Francis is like Solomon in this matter. He is asking the Church which mother it wants to be: The mother who is willing to see Jesus Christ split up, with each band of Christians preserving their piece with jealous care, or the mother who is willing to sacrifice as much as she possibly can to be sure that the Lord stays whole.

Count him on the side of the whole baby. "When we Christians speak of sharing in one Baptism, we affirm that we all—Catholics, Protestants and Orthodox—share in the experience of being called out of the merciless and alienating darkness to the encounter with the living God, full of mercy," he said during 2016's week of Prayer for Christian Unity. "Starting anew from Baptism means rediscovering the font of mercy, the font of hope for all, for no one is excluded from the mercy of God."

THE STAR AND THE CRESCENT

But what about those who don't share baptism with us? Pope Francis has also made interreligious dialogue a focus of his pontificate—again, following in the footsteps of his predecessors. With those of other religions, even monotheistic traditions, we share neither baptism nor the understanding of the God-made-man who makes baptism possible. What, then, is our responsibility to them—what does justice demand of us?

In *Lumen Fidei*, Pope Francis (with help from his predecessor, who wrote the first draft of the encyclical but resigned before promulgating it) says that all religious seekers are ultimately looking for God in his full self-revelation in the person of Jesus Christ. "An image of this seeking can be seen in the Magi, who were led to Bethlehem by the star," he writes. "Religious man is a wayfarer; he must be ready to let himself be led, to come out of himself and to find the God of perpetual surprises." The best way to understand the beauty of all religions is to draw closer to the one who that star shone on: Jesus Christ himself. "The more Christians immerse themselves in the circle of Christ's light, the more capable they become of understanding and accompanying the path of every man and woman towards God."[19]

Pope Francis's first answer to the barriers between religions has always been to open channels of communication. In his historic visit to the Holy Land in May 2014, he visited with Bartholomew I, Ecumenical Patriarch of Constantinople, to further Christian unity, and met with the Grand Mufti of Jerusalem to promote interreligious understanding.

When incidents like the ISIS beheading of Coptic Christians have become increasingly common, it can be hard to celebrate unreservedly the beauty of other religions. And yet, just as the closeness to Jesus allowed the families of the Coptic Christians to forgive their enemies, it can do the same for us.

On the plane ride from Istanbul to Rome, Pope Francis was asked about the rise of Islamophobia in the wake of terrorist attacks. "It's true that there has been a reaction to these acts of terrorism, not just in this region but in Africa as well: 'If this is Islam, it makes me angry!' So many Muslims feel offended," said Pope Francis. "They say: 'But that is not what we are. The Quran is a prophetic book of peace. This is not Islam.' I can understand this. And I sincerely believe that we cannot say all Muslims are terrorists, just as we cannot say that all Christians are fundamentalists—we also have fundamentalists among us, all religions have these small groups."

He called on Muslim leaders "to issue a clear condemnation against these kinds of groups. All religious leaders, scholars, clerics, intellectuals and politicians should do this," he said. "This way they hear it from their leaders' mouth. There needs to be international condemnation from Muslims across the world. It must be said, 'No, this is not what the Quran is about!'"

Then he added that Christianophobia is a much more dangerous phenomenon. He said: "On Christianophobia: It's true, I'm not going to soften my words, no. We Christians are being chased out of the Middle East." He described manifestations of Christianophobia, ways that Christians are discriminated against short of outright persecution: They have to pay extra taxes, or husbands and wives aren't allowed to live together. "It's as if they wished that there were no more Christians, that nothing remain of Christianity. In that region this is happening. It's true, it's first of all a result of terrorism, but when it's done diplomatically with white gloves, it's because there's something behind it. This is not good."[20]

Father Ragheed Ganni is an example of that painful reality that forces Christians out of the Middle East. After studying for the Chaldean priesthood in Rome, he returned to Iraq to help in the rebuilding after the Iraq War. But the violence only got worse, not better. Churches were increasingly bombed—sometimes while Sunday Mass was going on.

Father Don Kettle, a friend of his from seminary, shared what happened: "His church was blown up. Their house was blown up. He was saying Mass in the basement. He continued on." He recalled the story of Father Ragheed giving a group of terrified children their First Communion in the church's basement as gunfire raged outside. He told them the sound was fireworks in their honor.[21]

But "without Sunday, without the Eucharist, the Christians in Iraq cannot survive," said Father Ganni, again and again calling his flock to Sunday Mass. He told a Vatican Eucharistic Congress, "There are days when I feel frail and full of fear after seeing so many attacks on Iraqi Christians. But when, holding the Eucharist, I say, 'Behold the Lamb of God,' I feel his strength in me. When I hold the Host in my hands, it is really he who is holding me and all of us, challenging the terrorists and keeping us united in his boundless love."[22]

Father Ganni was shot dead in 2007. Most of his flock fled the country. Estimates suggest that the Christian population in Iraq was about 1.4 million before the 2003 U.S. led invasion ousted the religiously moderate Saddam Hussein, allowing religious extremists to take over. In February 2016 estimates put the Christian population between 260,000[23] and 350,000.[24]

Iraqi refugees are not sure where to go, because enemies such as ISIS are also on the move. In the ancient Iraq town of Maaloula—located thirty-four miles North of Damascus, Syria—the largely Christian population has spent the twenty-first century living in fear. The town came under siege by Islamic militants late in 2013 and was brought back under control by Syrian forces and a Hezbolla militia on April 14, 2014, the day after Palm Sunday. A sixty-two-year-old local man told reporters: "I saw people wearing al-Nusra headbands who started shooting at crosses." One gunman "put a pistol to the head of my neighbor and forced him to convert to Islam by obliging him to repeat, 'There is no God but Allah.' Afterward they joked, 'He's one of ours now.'"[25]

Other threats are working to "convert" Christians as well—for instance the threat that their daughters will be taken away from them. It is not surprising that, in the face of this persecution, many simply flee. It is hard to tell how many displaced people there are in the Middle East. In February of 2016, the best estimate of the number of Syrian refugees of various religions was 4.5 million. It is estimated that there were 1.1 million Christians in Syria in 2011; by February of 2015, a European Parliament resolution claimed more than 700,000 of them had fled.[26]

It is not just Christians who are fleeing, of course. The recent Middle East refugee crisis has a long, sad, interreligious history. On August 23, 2013, while attention was on the deadly chemical weapons attack that sparked Pope Francis's prayer vigil for peace, the United Nations reported that Syria had passed a "shameful milestone" that summer in its three-year civil war: one million Syrian children had become refugees, most of them under eleven years old.[27]

In his visit to the Holy Land, Pope Francis met with refugees in Bethany beyond the Jordan and prayed for "our beloved Syria, rent by nearly three years of civil strife which has led to countless deaths and forced millions to flee and seek exile in other countries. All of us want peace!"

WELCOMING STRANGERS

All of this raises the question of Pope Francis's desire for a more welcoming attitude toward immigrants. He has been especially insistent that Europeans should take responsibility for the Syrian refugees flooding into their borders. In an interview with an Argentinian radio station he said with some irony, "When there is an empty space, people try to fill it. If a country has no children, immigrants come in and take their place. I think of the birth rate in Italy, Portugal and Spain. I believe it is close to zero percent. So, if there are no children, there are empty spaces."[28]

He called on every Catholic parish in Europe to welcome the immigrants and said, "Facing the tragedy of tens of thousands of refugees—fleeing death by war and famine, and journeying towards the hope of life—the Gospel calls, asking of us to be close to the smallest and forsaken. To give them a concrete hope, and not just to tell them: 'Have courage, be patient!'"[29]

It is a message he has repeated everywhere he has gone—including America, where the influx of immigration comes from Latin America. One reason for his passion for immigrants is his personal history. "I am the son of emigrants and I belong to the emigration of 1929. It is true that, in those days there was work, but the ones from my family—who had jobs when they arrived in 1929—by 1932, with the economic crisis of the '30s, were out on the street, with nothing," Pope Francis said in an interview. "My grandfather bought a warehouse with 2,000 pesos which he borrowed, and my father, who was an accountant, was selling goods out of a basket. So they had the will to fight, to succeed.... I know about migration!"[30]

Another reason for his passion is his papal mission statement. The Church has to "go to the peripheries" and encounter those in trouble. The same is true when the peripheries come to you, he said in his first message for the World Day of Migrants and Refugees. "A change of attitude towards migrants and refugees is needed on the part of everyone," he said, "moving away from attitudes of defensiveness and fear, indifference and marginalization—all typical of a 'throwaway culture'—towards attitudes based on a culture of encounter, the only culture capable of building a better, more just and fraternal world."[31]

That is of course no small order. Throughout history, refugees have brought serious problems to the nations to which they immigrated. In

America, even Italian heritage organizations admit that statistics suggest that turn-of-the-century Italian immigrants had higher violent crime rates than other populations.[32] New research challenges the accuracy of those statistics, but it remains true that Americans at the time were certain that allowing so many immigrants into America was inviting trouble.[33] In the late nineteenth century, the American Protective Society was formed to try to push back against the flood of Catholic immigrants. At one time, the organization boasted more than two million members, according to the *Encyclopedia Britannica*.[34] Members took an elaborate oath promising not to do business with immigrants, particularly Catholic ones. The Ku Klux Klan in one of its incarnations saw Catholic and Jewish immigration as its main target, and by the 1920s the group claimed four million members—including President Warren Harding.[35]

The Catholic Church of the time responded with great energy and imagination to provide ways to welcome immigrants. Ethnic parishes helped ease immigrants' transition, sodalities helped them keep their Catholic faith, and fraternal organizations such as the Knights of Columbus helped teach the new immigrants how to be good, Catholic Americans. It was an uphill battle—the newcomers were from an underclass that existed in grinding poverty with little education. But the Church succeeded.

Pope Francis hopes for a similar response today. In his 2013 World Day of Migrants address, he said, "Not infrequently, the arrival of migrants, displaced persons, asylum-seekers, and refugees gives rise to suspicion and hostility. There is a fear that society will become less secure, that identity and culture will be lost, that competition for jobs will become stiffer and even that criminal activity will increase." The first task is "to break down stereotypes and to offer correct information in reporting the errors of a few as well as the honesty, rectitude and goodness of the majority."

His calls to be welcome to immigrants have become even more urgent as his pontificate has progressed. In his February 2016 visit to Mexico, he made a visit to the border town of Ciudad Juarez, where he celebrated Mass simultaneously with San Antonio Bishop Mark Seitz, whose Mass was conducted on the other side of the border in El Paso, Texas.

In April 2016, the Pope made headlines by bringing twelve Syrian refugees from Greece to Italy aboard the papal plane after visiting Lesbos, Greece. Pope Francis brought three families whose homes had been bombed in the Syrian war after meeting them in the Moria refugee camp.[36] I asked Bishop Seitz about the concerns many Americans have about Syrian refugees. In a time of terror, shouldn't we be more cautious about immigrants?

"Terrorism is a red herring," he said. "If a terrorist organization wants to send people, they have many means besides embedding them with Syrian refugees. The refugees sometimes take years to get to the United States, and they are fleeing from the very people the terrorists are most likely to be allied with. They aren't likely to help their enemies hide among them."

He said the task of the Catholic community is to do what our forebears did for our families: welcome and help these families transition. Pope Francis told US bishops in Washington, DC, how to treat the immigrants from Latin America. "Do not be afraid to welcome them. Offer them the warmth of the love of Christ and you will unlock the mystery of their heart. I am certain that, as so often in the past, these people will enrich America and its Church."[37]

Welcoming immigrants can grow the Church in more ways than one. Pope Francis has often quoted the early Church father Tertullian that "the blood of the martyrs is the seed of the Church." This is not just a mystical reality, he said. "Persecution breaks out, Christians are scattered and they preach the faith by their witness." Present-day martyrs, like those of the early Church, strengthen us by their witness in death. The witness of the faithful Christians we welcome into our communities—and the witness of Christians who reach out to those who do not share our faith—can strengthen us, too.

That witness is badly needed today. Imagine if more of us had the faith of those Coptic martyrs. The most heartbreaking cry for mercy in the stories I read came from a little girl: Fifi, the daughter of the martyr Maged Shehata, who spoke with Jonathan Rashad. "My father died like a lion," she said. "He did not bow his head down. ISIS has no religion or mercy. I am now from the city of the martyrs. The city of the brave lions. May God forgive the killers. We don't have hatred towards them—this is Christianity. God forgives the sinners; so shall we."[38]

May God grant Pope Francis's prayer and give more of us the faith of that little girl.

CHAPTER EIGHT

Big Green Problems

> "Blessed are the meek, for they will inherit the earth."
> —Matthew 5:5 (NRSV)

Pope Francis's second encyclical, *Laudato Sí*, was a masterstroke delivered at a perfect cultural moment capable of drawing the world nearer to the Church and drawing the faithful people of the Church to serve the world in a beautiful new way.

Or at least, it should have been.

Pope Francis's strategy from the beginning has been to identify and widen openings for dialogue with the world. He wanted to show the world how relevant to their lives the Church is. In dedicating an encyclical to the environment, Pope Francis was showing Catholics how to start a conversation with the larger culture by engaging one of its favorite issues and transforming it.

He was showing Catholics how to say, "Yes, concern for the environment is important, and urgent, and our care for nature has to be real and expansive—so expansive that it protects *human* nature from pollution, too." He was doing with the virtue of environmental concern what the gay marriage movement had done with the culture's new openness to sex: forcing it to its logical conclusion. If we already accept sex without boundaries, why stop at same-sex marriage? If we already say we should protect the ecosystem and stop needlessly killing animals, why not protect the ecosystem of our bodies and stop needlessly killing the unborn?

He was also showing the larger culture that the Catholic faith had fresh, relevant things to say about issues the larger culture found important. It was a moment when God's faithful people could rally around their pope and show the freshness and relevance of the Gospel to the world. They could join with their non-Catholic neighbors in the common cause of protecting our common home. When we make common cause with others, good things happen. They let down their defenses. We are more open to each other. They might even get a glimpse of the joy of the Gospel, and we might even find the joy of evangelization.

So why didn't it work out that way?

LAUDATO...NO.

In fact, after the release of *Laudato Sí* in May of 2015, the pope's "favorability rating," as measured by Gallup, fell. The polling company asks about one thousand people the question, "Please say if you have a favorable or unfavorable opinion of Pope Francis." In February 2014, 76 percent said favorable. By July 2015, only 59 percent had a favorable opinion—a 17-point drop.

People of all stripes grew less favorable toward the pope, including both self-described liberals and moderates, but according to Gallup, "the drop in the pope's favorable rating is driven by a decline among Catholics and political conservatives, two groups that have been ardent supporters of the modern papacy." The percentage of Catholics favorable to the pope took a 21-point drop, from 73 percent to 52 percent.[1]

What happened? Why were the groups most likely to support a pope the most likely to sour on Francis? One answer is that the rave reviews Pope Francis was getting left this group cold. They increasingly viewed Pope Francis as someone who was soft on the social issues they held dear and a passionate proponent of economic and environmental theories they found dubious.

I know how they felt. In my work in the Catholic media, I was hearing repeatedly from Catholics who had deep misgivings about Pope Francis and the direction he was taking the Church. Many of the worries centered around rumors that the pope was colluding with a group of like-minded cardinals who wanted to reform the Church.

The rumors were given life by a biography of Belgian Cardinal Godfried Daneels and Austen Ivereigh's biography on Pope Francis, *The Great Reformer*. Both books reported on a group called the St. Gallen Club, which included Cardinal Daneels and the late Cardinal Carlo Martini of Milan. Ivereigh mentioned that Cardinal Bergoglio was acquainted with the group in the years leading up to the conclave that elected him. His narrative allowed for some overlap between the "the St. Gallen Club" and the conclave's "Team Bergoglio," Ivereigh's name for the electors who coalesced around the future Pope Francis in the conclave that elected him.[2] But in his telling, the two groups were by no means a single reality with a single aim.

However, it wasn't just Catholics who follow Vatican news who were growing wary of Pope Francis in 2014. The year 2014 saw a number of false reports about the "people's pope" surface, spread through Internet memes or in clickbait stories on sites that specialize in sensationalism.

Some were benign: One false report said that Pope Francis sneaks out of his Vatican apartment at night to serve the homeless. Others were manipulative: One showed Pope Francis's picture and falsely attributed this quote to him: "The Church no longer believes in a literal hell where people suffer. This doctrine is incompatible with the infinite love of God."

A satirical news report describing Francis presiding over a radical "Vatican III" meeting of bishops that was changing fundamental doctrines of the Church was taken seriously by some people. Even when these stories were obviously false, they added to the Black Legend of Francis, the pope who everyone knew was soft on Catholic doctrine.

Some of the misunderstandings were Francis's own fault. He sat down several times to be interviewed by an atheist friend of his, the retired journalist Eugenio Scalfari, a founder of the newspaper *La Repubblica*. Scalfari was eighty-nine when he first interviewed the pope in 2013; his final interview was published two years later, in 2015. Each time the former editor of *La Repubblica* neither recorded the pope nor even took notes.[3] And each time, Scalfari published stories that attributed words to Pope Francis that sounded a little like things the pope had said elsewhere but with subtle differences that had significant implications.

After his first interview in 2013, Scalfari confessed that he used "his own words" to express the positions he attributed to the pope.[4] The text of that interview was published on the Vatican website nonetheless.[5] In 2015, Vatican spokesman Father Federico Lombardi said Scalfari's newest interview was "in no way reliable."[6] By then Scalfari had published a story quoting Francis promising to use the Synod on the Family to change the Church's practice regarding divorce and Communion.

Papal Misunderstandings

If Scalfari's stories represented one kind of journalistic malfeasance, another was much more common: Stories that inadvertently showed that secular news reporters know a lot less about the Catholic faith than politics or sports—or at any rate that they are a lot less willing to fact-check what they write about the faith. Combine that with a desire to make a progressive hero of Pope Francis, and you had a steady stream of stories that misrepresented the pope and cast suspicion on him in some Catholics' eyes.

Many of these had at least a passing connection to his thoughts on nature and the environment. For instance, on October 27, 2014, Pope Francis spoke to the Academy of Sciences and said "evolution in nature is not opposed to the notion of Creation," then added, with his typical flair, that God is not a "magician" who creates with a "magic wand" but rather "created beings and left them to develop according to the internal laws that he gave each one, so that they would develop, and reach their fullness."[7]

The remarks created a sensation. The Daily Beast's headline said with surprise: "Even the pope isn't a hard-core Creationist," which is a true statement—about Pope Pius XII (whose encyclical *Humani Generis* allowed for evolutionary theories in 1950) and every pope since. *U.S. News and World Report*'s headline said: "Pope Francis Backs the Big Bang Theory, Evolution," apparently unaware that the Big Bang Theory was originally proposed by a Catholic priest, Belgian Father Georges Lemaître, in 1931. National Public Radio announced, "Pope Says God Not 'A Magician, with a Magic Wand,'" but didn't mention that the *Catechism of the Catholic Church* says essentially the same thing too (*CCC* 283).

Another embarrassing news story came in December, conflating Pope Francis quotes with decades-old words of Pope Paul VI to a distraught child who had just lost his dog. The news made the front page of the *New York Times*, under the headline "Dogs in Heaven? Pope Francis Leaves Pearly Gates Open." The lead sentence compounded the error by connecting several hot-button issues that were subject to papal misunderstandings: "Pope Francis has given hope to gays, unmarried couples and advocates of the Big Bang theory," reported the *Times*, "Now, he has endeared himself to dog lovers, animal rights activists and vegans."[8]

Pope Francis said the adulatory news coverage made him uncomfortable. "I don't like the ideological interpretations, a certain 'mythology of Pope Francis,'" he said. "When it is said, for example, that he goes out of the Vatican at night to walk and to feed the homeless on Via Ottaviano. It has never crossed my mind. If I'm not wrong, Sigmund Freud said that in every idealization there is an aggression. Depicting the pope to be a sort of superman, a type of star, seems offensive to me. The pope is a man who laughs, cries, sleeps calmly, and has friends like everyone. A normal person."[9]

He also said he doesn't like the cries of "Francis! Francis!" that greet him in St. Peter's Square. "Where was Jesus? I should have preferred to hear you cry: 'Jesus, Jesus is Lord, and he is in our midst!' From now on enough of 'Francis,' just 'Jesus!'"[10] (In fact, he has attempted on several occasions to direct crowds to do just that.)

WOLVES AND RABBITS

If 2014 was the year the media misunderstood the pope, 2015 was the year many Catholics misunderstood him. It began in January when he disappointed two very different groups of Catholics. In a visit to the Philippines, he strongly reiterated the Church's teaching on contraception and then later attempted to make the teaching more palatable to secular critics.

"I think of Blessed Paul VI," he told a January 16 meeting of families in Manila. "At a time when the problem of population growth was being raised, he had the courage to defend openness to life in families." Francis mentioned the encyclical *Humanae Vitae* (On the Regulation of Birth), which reiterated Church teaching against contraception and said it showed the "broader vision" of Paul VI. "He looked at the peoples of the earth and he saw this threat of families being destroyed for lack of children," Francis said. "Paul VI was courageous; he was a good pastor and he warned his flock of the wolves who were coming."[11]

The remark was an apparent reference to the four warnings Pope Paul VI issued in his landmark encyclical against birth control. He said the widespread use of contraception would result, on the personal level, in a decline in sexual morality and an increasing disrespect for women and, on a societal level, would lead to abuse by governments and a tendency by science and medicine to feel they have "unlimited domination" over the human body. Scholars such as Janet Smith and Mary Eberstadt have spelled out how artificial contraception has had precisely the ill effects the pope feared.[12]

The reaction was swift. "The news that Pope Francis has strongly defended the Church's ban on artificial birth control left me, in a word, devastated. I had hoped for so much more from this man," wrote Margery Eagan on the Crux website, then affiliated with the *Boston Globe*, on January 17, 2015. "Pope Francis left me feeling foolish for even hoping that he'd somehow see his way to ending the Church's completely indefensible contraception ban," she added. "Mostly, I just feel sad."[13]

Michael Coren's stronger reaction took a little longer. The Canadian talk-show host and author of *Why Catholics Are Right* announced in the spring that he had left the Catholic Church and explained in a May 2 interview with the *National Post* that he objected to the Church's teaching on homosexuality. "Francis has also gone to the Philippines and referred to 'gender theory,' which is Catholic code really for same-sex issues, and compared it to the Hitler Youth. The Catholic Church is not going to change its teaching. Believe me, the Catholic Church cannot." That wasn't the only reason he left, though. "There's more than that," Coren added on a video of the interview the *Post* included with the story online, and said that "the teaching on contraception" was another reason he was leaving.[14]

Ironically, in the same January 19 papal plane interview that offended Coren, another group of Catholics found a very different reason to be angry at the pope. German-language journalist Christoph Schmidt challenged him for his strong backing of the Church's teaching on contraception in a Third World country. "The majority of Filipinos think that the enormous growth of the Filipino population is one of the most important reasons for the immense poverty in the country," he said, "and the Catholic position regarding contraception appears to be one of the few questions on which a great number of people in the Philippines do not agree with the Church."

Pope Francis mentioned an example he had already used of a woman expecting her eighth child after already having had seven children by Caesarean section. "This is a form of irresponsibility," he said. He said that for such a person to say, "I trust God," is no answer. "God gives you the means; be responsible. Some people believe that—pardon my language—in order to be good Catholics, we should be like rabbits. No. Responsible parenthood. This is clear and it is the reason why in the

Church there are marriage groups, there are experts in this area, there are pastors, and people are trying."[15]

Of course, he was right: Responsible parenthood is a crucial part of the Church's teaching. But his word choice sounded harsh to Catholics who have large families. I confess I was one of them: I have nine children, born through enough sacrifice for my wife and myself that some might label us irresponsible, too. A good friend who has six children changed his Facebook profile picture to Bugs Bunny to ironically celebrate his own rabbit-like tendencies.

The pope must have realized he should have worded his remarks differently because he went out of his way to revise and extend them twice. The first time was a few days later at his January 21 general audience. "It gives consolation and hope to see so many large families that welcome children as a gift from God," he said. "They know that every child is a blessing." He also refuted once again the opinion that "the birth of many children are among the causes of poverty."[16]

On February 11, 2015, he went further, saying that a society "which does not love being surrounded by children, which considers them above all a worry, a weight, a risk, is a depressed society." He noted that Europe falls short of a replacement birthrate, and explained why. Yes, he said, parenting "must be responsible, as the Encyclical *Humanae Vitae* of Blessed Pope Paul VI also teaches, but having many children cannot automatically be an irresponsible choice. Not to have children is a selfish choice."[17]

So, what was the rabbits comment all about? It seems that Pope Francis got caught betwixt and between in remarks to two different audiences. He had just praised the courage of Paul VI for his teaching on birth control in a speech to enthusiastic Filipino Catholics. When challenged about his remarks by European journalists on the plane ride home, he felt it necessary to explain. By saying that you don't have to "be like rabbits" to be a good Catholic, he wasn't saying, "Too many people are having too many babies." He was saying, "Too many people dismiss the Church's teaching on contraception as impractical." And that needed to be said.

Contraception comments would continue to challenge the Pope. On the plane ride back from Mexico in February of 2016 he seemed to greenlight the use of contraceptives as a "lesser evil" than abortion in countries ravaged by the Zika virus. Two months later he put to rest the implication that he would allow contraception with a vigorous defense of *Humanae Vitae* in his exhortation on marriage.[18]

Another moment that turned off would-be fans of Pope Francis came during his six-day trip to South America. The visit was an inspiring show of papal solidarity with the South American people, but it generated controversy early on when Evo Morales, the president of Bolivia, presented the pope with a crucifix made out of a Soviet hammer and sickle symbol. Waves of media confusion followed. First, there were eagerly shared memes of the pope's disapproving look when he saw the central sign of Christian salvation turned into a political statement. Then came a second wave of images, taken a few moments later, showing Pope Francis's smile when receiving the gift. Then there were conflicting reports about whether the pope had left the gift behind or kept it.

The pope himself laid the matter to rest on the plane ride home. "I would qualify it as protest art that can in some cases be offensive; in some cases," he said. Then he added that it was made in the style of a Jesuit artist whose artwork had caught the attention decades ago of Jesuit Superior Pedro Arrupe, who sent a letter to all Jesuits ordering the rejection of Marxism. Four years later, he added, the Vatican cracked down on Marxist versions of liberation theology.

He mentioned other honors he received from President Morales in addition to the crucifix and said, "I thought that this comes from the people of Bolivia—I prayed about this and thought about it—and if I take them to the Vatican they will end up in a museum where nobody will see them. So, I decided to leave them to Our Lady of Copacabana, the Mother of Bolivia.... However, I am taking the sculpture of Christ with me."[19]

In other words, Pope Francis handled the gift diplomatically but firmly. He thanked the president, corrected the Marxist sentiment behind it, and then took it back with him "where nobody will see" it.

That didn't stop critics from defining Pope Francis as a Marxist because of the gift. Dennis Prager wrote in *National Review*, "The pope's acceptance of Morales's gift—along with his attacks on capitalism during his Latin American tour—further confirms one of the most troubling moral developments of our time: The Roman Catholic Church is currently led by a man whose social, political, and economic views have been shaped by leftism more than by any other religious or moral system."[20]

LIVING THE BEATITUDES

And so it was that when Pope Francis gave the Church a big, beautiful, challenging encyclical in *Laudato Sí: On Care for our Common Home*, many American Catholics were primed to be wary of it. It is a brilliant work—a work that takes the opening the world has offered through its concern for the environment and uses it to passionately demand radical conversion.

This is the pope who once said: "With these two things you have the action plan: the Beatitudes and Matthew 25. You do not need to read anything else." *Laudato Sí* can be read as a detailed, bold application of the Beatitudes, found in Mathew 5:3–12 to modern life, refusing to soft pedal the Gospel life or the failings of contemporary society.

The first beatitude says, "Blessed are the poor in spirit," literally, "How fortunate those who beg for their life's very breath!"[21] *Laudato Sí* says to treat all of creation as "a gift from the outstretched hand of the Father of all."[22]

The second beatitude says, "The meek shall inherit the earth;" *Laudato Sí* insists that human beings accept the world and live within its parameters, that "rather than a problem to be solved, the world is a joyful mystery to be contemplated with gladness and praise."[23]

The whole encyclical is a plea to the people of the world to "hunger and thirst for righteousness." As *Laudato Sí* puts it, "Many things have to change course, but it is we human beings above all who need to change."[24]

It even addresses specific hot-button issues in a way that conforms to the beatitudes. It applies Jesus's "Blessed are they who mourn," to abortion, saying, "How can we genuinely teach the importance of concern for other vulnerable beings, however troublesome or inconvenient they may be, if we fail to protect a human embryo?" The pope adds that the loss of the ability to mourn human life makes other sensitivities "wither away."[25]

It ties "Blessed are the pure at heart" to a number of issues, saying, "Thinking that we enjoy absolute power over our bodies turns, often subtly, into thinking that we enjoy absolute power over creation," and adds that "valuing one's own body in its femininity or masculinity is necessary."[26]

On war, *Laudato Sí* describes just how "blessed are the peacemakers." Peace "is much more than the absence of war," it says, describing peace as "a balanced lifestyle together with a capacity for wonder" far from "constant noise, interminable and nerve-wracking distractions, or the cult of appearances."[27]

Finally, the last beatitude in Luke says, "Blessed are you when people hate you, and when they exclude and insult you, and denounce your name as evil on account of the son of man," and *Laudato Sí* brought plenty of that to Pope Francis, too.

George F. Will summed up the pope's theories as "Pope Francis's Fact-Free Flamboyance" in a column focused on *Laudato Sí* in *The Washington Post* September 18, 2015.[28] Damon Linker at *The Week* tried to explain "Why Conservatives Are Going Nuclear on Pope Francis."[29]

But they weren't the only critics. At *Slate*, William Saletan cautioned that, despite his encyclical on the environment, "Pope Francis isn't the liberal rock star American Catholics think he is."[30] At *Salon*, Kathleen Geier would warn: "The Argentinian pontiff has earned plaudits from the left. Don't be fooled by the hype."[31]

Skeptics of global warming theories—and there are many—thought that it was inappropriate for the pope to weigh in on the question at all. Pope Francis is careful at first to say that "a scientifically determinable cause cannot be assigned"[32] to global warming, but then he later emphatically denounces "the warming caused by huge consumption on the part of some rich countries."[33] Ultimately, the document itself does not consider its take on climate science definitive: "On many concrete questions, the Church has no reason to offer a definitive opinion; she knows that honest debate must be encouraged among experts while respecting divergent views," it says.[34]

But Pope Francis was not the first pope to urge international attention to curb global warming. Benedict did so on several occasions, telling his diplomatic corps in 2009, "How can we not mention the food crisis and global warming, which make it even more difficult for those living in some of the poorest parts of the planet to have access to nutrition and water?"[35]

It was also an occasional theme of St. John Paul II, who included his concerns for climate change in his 2001 pastoral plan for the Church in Oceania (Australia, New Zealand, and surrounding regions), warning that the people of Polynesia and Micronesia face "a very uncertain future, not only because of large-scale emigration but also because of rising sea levels caused by global warming. For them, climate change is very much more than a question of economics."[36]

Techno-logic

It therefore was not the focus on climate change that was the most revolutionary aspect of *Laudato Sí*. It was the pope's relentless insistence that his readers address a fundamental problem with contemporary culture that we might not want to focus on: The dark triumph of technology and consumerism in almost every aspect of our lives. "A constant flood of new consumer goods can baffle the heart and prevent us from cherishing each thing and each moment," he writes. "To be serenely present to each reality, however small it may be, opens us to much greater horizons of understanding and personal fulfilment."[37]

You can see how technology cocoons us on a typical summer workday. We go from air-conditioned house to air-conditioned car to air-conditioned office. On the way, we listen to a satellite radio station customized to our particular taste. We get coffees for the office in a drink holder from the drive through. At work, we deal with coworkers mostly through e-mail—even when they are sitting five yards away. We take a break and check in at our favorite opinion website, whose writers' beliefs match, and rarely challenge, our own. On the way home, we buy a package of cheese shredded for us that we will need for dinner; we scan it ourselves and swipe our card. After dinner at home, we stream a movie on Netflix while we order batteries, pens, and deodorant from Amazon on our phone. The kids play video games on the Xbox or Snapchat with friends on their tablets. Each family member is in a separate world.

The day requires minimal contact with other human beings and zero contact with nature; it also takes a huge amount of energy to fuel it and leaves behind waste nearly equal in weight to what we consume. It is all in one way benign, and in another way deeply troubling. It is benign in that we don't really commit any real sin in any of it; it is troubling in that it has heedlessly left waste in our wake while subtly stripping us of the ability to have authentic encounters with others. It has severed us from the primal meaning of the world around us.

"Technology tends to absorb everything into its ironclad logic," writes Pope Francis. "In the most radical sense of the term, power is its motive—a lordship over all."[38] He would continue on that theme quite a bit throughout the year, giving great, practical advice to families: Put smart phones away at dinner; rediscover one another and rediscover nature.

But some of the people who needed to hear it most—and could do the most to apply the message in new and exciting ways—never really heard it. All those misunderstandings made it nearly impossible to hear what the pope was really saying. As summer ended and September arrived, it was an open question: What kind of reception would Pope Francis receive when he visited the United States?

The world would soon find out.

Chapter Nine

Land of the Free

"Repay to Caesar what belongs to Caesar and to God
what belongs to God."
—Matthew 22:21

And so we come to Pope Francis's visit to the United States in 2015. This book has been looking at issues in the order in which they arose in his pontificate. Each one of them seemed to come up again in 2015 in America, making the visit a good way to sum up where we have been so far. The visit was also filled with beautiful examples of Pope Francis's culture of encounter—the subject of the last chapter. But first we need to look at one last issue: Pope Francis's vision of religious freedom in an increasingly secular West.

Yes, he would also repeat his calls for environmental solutions—but his calls for religious freedom were the thematic center of gravity in the trip. The first thing Pope Francis did in official remarks on American soil on September 23, 2015, was to plead with the president of the United States for religious liberty. After expressing his gratitude and outlining his schedule, he said Catholics and other people of good will ask that their nation "respect their deepest concerns and their right to religious liberty. That freedom remains one of America's most precious possessions."

He would repeat the plea again and again, from the US Congress to the United Nations to Independence Hall in Philadelphia. Religious freedom would also become a major theme of his unscheduled meetings with the Little Sisters of the Poor, who have taken legal action against the Obama Administration for their right to conscience with regard to health care insurance—and with Kim Davis, the court clerk who went to jail rather than allow her signature to be used on marriage certificates for same-sex couples.

THE POPE COMES TO AMERICA

The image of a Pope Francis traveling to the great cities of the world's last remaining superpower to demand religious freedom from America has a built-in drama to it. Given the place that America has taken in the imagination of the world, "The pope comes to America" has a ring to it that is something like "the Prophet goes to Babylon" or "Paul visits Athens."

In 2015, the drama was even greater. To situate the papal visit in a timeline of a rapidly changing America, consider this: Pope Francis arrived in Washington, DC, seventy years after the bombing of Hiroshima by the United States, forcing the Japanese to surrender and ending World War II. He arrived fifty years after the Selma-to-Montgomery March for civil rights, forty years after the founding of global technology dominator Microsoft, and twenty years after the Oklahoma City bombing.

More to the point, he arrived in the very year America seemed to be undergoing fundamental changes—many of them in the span of a single month. On the ninth of July, the US attorney general announced that same-sex couples with marriage licenses would thereafter enjoy all the federal benefits of married couples, due to the Supreme Court's decision two weeks earlier.[1] Bruce Jenner's iconic image as the muscular athlete promising a "Breakfast of Champions" on the Wheaties box reappeared, post–sex change, in the July 2015 *Vanity Fair* as a busty female figure in a corset, over the cover line "Call Me Caitlyn."

All Ten Commandments seemed to be up for grabs in America in 2015.

"You shall not have strange gods before me?" On July 25, seven hundred people gathered in Detroit for the unveiling of a gigantic Satanic statue in what was billed as the "largest public satanic ceremony in history."[2]

"Remember to keep holy the Lord's Day?" The US Postal Service was busy delivering packages for Amazon every Sunday, and (according to Bloomberg Businessweek) was making deals that July with more companies for Sunday delivery.[3]

"Honor your father and your mother?" On July 28, 2015, the *Today* show offered a report teaching families "How to deal with kids that bully their parents."[4]

"You shall not kill?" On July 14, 2015, David Daleiden at the Center for Medical Progress released the first of a series of underground videos he recorded documenting Planned Parenthood officials making light of the lives of the unborn and offering to sell their body parts.[5]

"You shall not commit adultery?" On July 15, 2015, the website of Ashley Madison, a service that helps connect people looking to cheat on their spouses was hacked and the names of its millions of users exposed.[6]

So much about America was going in the opposite direction from Pope Francis. It was clear that the culture in America, so long allied with the principles of its Christian majority, was becoming increasingly hostile to what Christians have traditionally believed. The direction America was taking was one that Catholics couldn't go—but the country was becoming more likely to compel religious citizens into coming along.

Chicago's Cardinal Francis George had first raised the alarm about religious freedom in March 2009. In an unusual YouTube message to Catholics after meeting with President Obama, then-president of the U.S. Conference of Catholic Bishops Cardinal George reported that the Obama Administration had announced plans to remove a conscience protection rule from the Department of Health and Human Services. "No government should come between an individual person and God— that's what America is supposed to be about," he said. "As Catholic bishops and American citizens, we are deeply concerned that such an action on the government's part would be the first step in moving our country from democracy to despotism."[7]

Bishop William Lori raised the alarm again in Congressional testimony in 2011. He was the Bishop of Bridgeport at the time; he is now the Cardinal Archbishop of Baltimore and has been the Supreme Chaplain of the Knights of Columbus since 2005. "The Bishops of the United States have watched with increasing alarm as this great national legacy of religious liberty…has been subject to ever more frequent assault and ever more rapid erosion," he said. His testimony centered on a Health and Human Services regulation mandating that Church organizations provide health insurance coverage that violates Church teaching against contraception and abortion. "There is an exception for certain religious employers," said Lori, "but to borrow from Sr. Carol Keehan of the Catholic Health Association, it is so incredibly narrow that it would cover only the 'parish housekeeper.'"[8]

In 2012, the Church ratcheted up its defense of religious freedom, proclaiming a "Fortnight of Freedom," a yearly celebration of religious liberty that begins on the June 21 and lasts until July 4's celebration of the Declaration of Independence. The two-week time period includes a plethora of martyrs to religious freedom—St. Thomas More and St. John Fisher, St. John the Baptist, Saints Peter and Paul, and the First Martyrs of the Church of Rome. As Cardinal Francis George famously put it in May 2012, "I expected to die in bed, my successor will die in prison and his successor will die a martyr in the public square. His successor will pick up the shards of a ruined society and slowly help rebuild civilization, as the Church has done so often in human history."[9]

By 2015's Fortnight for Freedom, the Church had even more reason for alarm. A wedding photographer in New Mexico and wedding cake bakers in Colorado and Oregon were among those who had already been penalized for refusing their services at same-sex weddings, which they objected to on religious grounds.[10] In June, the Supreme Court's *Obergefell v. Hodges* decision guaranteed that religious liberty fights over same-sex marriage would go national.

Justice Anthony Kennedy in his majority opinion suggested that the decision would not impinge on religious freedom. "Finally, it must be emphasized that religions, and those who adhere to religious doctrines, may continue to advocate with utmost, sincere conviction that, by divine precepts, same-sex marriage should not be condoned."[11] Chief Justice John Roberts, in his dissent to the decision, directly addressed Kennedy: "The majority graciously suggests that religious believers may continue to 'advocate' and 'teach' their views of marriage. The First Amendment guarantees, however, the freedom to 'exercise' religion."[12]

So it was inevitable that religious liberty would become a focus of Pope Francis's visit to America. He came as a man of enormous moral authority who had enthusiastic popular support. As he emerged from "Shepherd One" onto a windy Andrews Air Force Base tarmac, shouts of "Francisco! Francisco!" filled the air—the first Latin American Pope's first greeting in America was in Spanish. As he shook hands with President Obama and his family, who made an unprecedented trip out onto the runway to greet this particular visiting dignitary, the shouts changed to "Ho, ho! Hey, hey! Welcome to the U.S.A.!"

The jolly spirit continued at the White House welcoming ceremony on the South Lawn of the White House the next day. Almost every line of both the president's and the pope's speeches was greeted with wild applause by the eleven thousand guests present; for instance, when President Obama said: "You remind us that people are only truly free when they can practice their faith freely."

"Here in the United States, we cherish religious liberty. It was the basis for so much of what brought us together," the president added. Noting religious persecution around the world, he said, "We stand with you in defense of religious freedom and interfaith dialogue, knowing that people everywhere must be able to live out their faith free from fear and free from intimidation."[13]

Pope Francis's speech had two goals with regard to religious liberty: First, to assure the president that Catholics don't discriminate against others and, second, to ask that they be treated likewise. He said, "American Catholics are committed to building a society which is truly tolerant and inclusive, to safeguarding the rights of individuals and communities, and to rejecting every form of unjust discrimination." Then he took the call for religious liberty one step further, however, saying, "All are called to be vigilant, precisely as good citizens, to preserve and defend that freedom from everything that would threaten *or compromise* it."[14]

SURPRISE MEETINGS

One thing he meant by "uncompromised" religious freedom became clear later that afternoon, when he made an unscheduled stop at a religious house of the Little Sisters of the Poor, a religious congregation that was in the midst of a legal battle with the Obama Administration.

The Little Sisters of the Poor is a worldwide order of religious sisters who care for the elderly. They are taking a stand for religious liberty against the Health and Human Services regulation which asks them either to violate their consciences or pay massive fines. With the help of the Beckett Fund for Religious Liberty, a nonprofit public-interest law firm, they filed for an exemption from the regulation in the federal district court in Denver, Colorado, in 2012. That initial effort failed, and they took their battle all the way to the Supreme Court, insisting that the kinds of exemptions to the health care regulations that the federal government gives to corporations like Exxon and Pepsi were being unjustly withheld from them.[15]

The pope's visit was an important symbolic show of solidarity with their cause. It was also a shot in the arm for the sisters who were there. The visit "gave us a lot of moral support and confirmed we are on the right track with the lawsuit as far as the church is concerned," Sister Constance Veit told NBC.[16]

Two other meetings also sent important messages about Pope Francis's understanding of religious freedom. He met with a former student of his, a homosexual man who has kept in touch with the pope, and he met with Kentucky court clerk Kim Davis. Neither visit was initiated by the Holy Father, so neither is as significant as the Little Sisters of the Poor visit, but both are telling.

Yayo Grassi, the former student, brought his partner, Iwan Bagus, and a small group to see the pope at the Vatican Embassy in Washington. Pope Francis warmly embraced him. Father Jorge Bergoglio taught at the Jesuit school Grassi attended in Santa Fe, Argentina, in the 1960s. "He was an extraordinary teacher and a great mentor," Grassi told the *Washington Post*. "He kept pushing my horizons, to oblige me to keep looking. He asked me to put on the skin of my fellow man, to feel their pain."[17]

Grassi, a sixty-seven-year-old who runs his own catering business in Washington, said he contacted Pope Francis when he learned his old teacher would be visiting America, and the pope agreed to arrange a meeting.

The next day, Pope Francis met with Kim Davis, the court clerk who was jailed over a same-sex marriage dispute in Kentucky. Ryan Anderson, the editor of *Public Discourse*, explained the much misunderstood Kim Davis case in *The New York Times*. "Because each marriage license issued by the clerk's office bore her name and title," he wrote, "Ms. Davis concluded that her religious beliefs meant she could not have her office issue licenses to same-sex couples. So she had the office stop issuing them entirely"—to all couples.[18] When she refused to change course after a court order, she was jailed for contempt of court.

Davis's lawyer, Mathew D. Staver, said that she and her husband, Joe, visited the pope in the Vatican embassy by car on Thursday, September 24, the pope's last day in Washington. He said Pope Francis gave them rosaries and said, "Stay strong."[19]

Davis was interviewed on ABC News about the meeting. "I put my hand out and he reached and he grabbed it, and I hugged him and he hugged me," Davis said. "And he said, 'Thank you for your courage.'

I had tears coming out of my eyes. I'm just a nobody, so it was really humbling to think he would want to meet or know me."[20]

The Vatican at first refused to confirm or deny that the meeting took place, but a week later, Father Federico Lombardi acknowledged the meeting in a statement.[21]

In the two meetings, Pope Francis was showing with his personal witness what he had told President Obama. People of faith do not discriminate, and we ought not be discriminated against. His embrace of Grassi is exactly what the *Catechism of the Catholic Church* asks when it says homosexuals "must be accepted with respect, compassion, and sensitivity. Every sign of unjust discrimination in their regard should be avoided." His embrace of Davis points to what the *Catechism* teaches about religious freedom: "Nobody may be forced to act against his convictions, nor is anyone to be restrained from acting in accordance with his conscience in religious matters in private or in public, alone or in association with others, within due limits" (*CCC* 2106).

On the airplane on the way back to Rome, Pope Francis was asked about Davis's case. "Holy Father, you visited the Little Sisters of the Poor, and we were told that you wanted to show your support for the Sisters, also in their court case," Terry Morgan of *ABC News* asked the pope. "Holy Father, do you also support those individuals, including government officials, who say they cannot in good conscience, their personal conscience, comply with certain laws or carry out their duties as government officials, for example in issuing marriage licenses to same-sex couples? Would you support those as claims of religious freedom?"

"I can't foresee every possible case of conscientious objection. But yes, I can say conscientious objection is a right, and enters into every human right," he said. "Every legal system should provide for conscientious objection because it is a right, a human right."

Morgan followed up by asking again, "Would that include government officials as well?"

"It is a human right," answered the pope, "and if a government official is human person, he enjoys that right."[22]

WHEN FREEDOMS CLASH

Pope Francis's defense of religious freedom in America couldn't have been stronger. But he also acknowledged the difficulties that religious freedom entails. His official speeches addressed some of the complications that arise in a pluralistic society with competing religious visions.

He opened his address to Congress by quoting the national anthem, calling America "the land of the free and the home of the brave." In his speech he suggested bravery is needed in the face of real freedom. "A delicate balance is required to combat violence perpetrated in the name of a religion, an ideology or an economic system, while also safeguarding religious freedom, intellectual freedom and individual freedoms."

He structured the speech around the figures of four great Americans who got that "delicate balance" right. In his conclusion, he proposed them as models of religious freedom, saying, "A nation can be considered great when it defends liberty as Lincoln did; when it fosters a culture which enables people to 'dream' of full rights for all their brothers and sisters, as Martin Luther King sought to do; when it strives for justice and the cause of the oppressed, as Dorothy Day did by her tireless work; the fruit of a faith which becomes dialogue and sows peace in the contemplative style of Thomas Merton."[23]

In each of his official speeches, he called for urgent action to help the environment, assist the poor, and promote peace. In his speech to the General Assembly of the United Nations, he said religious freedom was just as important. "Government leaders must do everything possible to ensure that all can have the minimum spiritual and material means needed to live in dignity and to create and support a family," he said. "In practical terms, this absolute minimum has three names: lodging, labor, and land; and one spiritual name: spiritual freedom, which includes religious freedom, the right to education and all other civil rights."[24]

In front of Independence Hall in Philadelphia, where forty thousand people came to hear Pope Francis speak, the visuals couldn't have been more perfect. Steps away from the place where America's founders signed the Declaration of Independence, he said, "Various forms of modern tyranny seek to suppress religious freedom, or...try to reduce it to a subculture without right to a voice in the public square."

Pope Francis argued that religious belief isn't an eccentricity to be tolerated; it is a fundamental building block of civil society. "Religious freedom certainly means the right to worship God, individually and in community, as our consciences dictate," he said. "But religious liberty, by its nature, transcends places of worship and the private sphere of individuals and families. Because religion itself, the religious dimension, is not a subculture; it is part of the culture of every people and every nation."

After listing ways religious people build a culture, he reminded the audience what the result is when systems that imagine "no religion, too"[25] take charge. "We need but look at history...especially the history of the last century, to see the atrocities perpetrated by systems which claimed to build one or another 'earthly paradise' by dominating peoples, subjecting them to apparently indisputable principles and denying them any kind of rights."

At the home of the Liberty Bell, speaking from the same lectern Abraham Lincoln used to read the Gettysburg Address, he concluded by issuing a kind of rallying cry for religious freedom in America. "Let us preserve freedom. Let us cherish freedom. Freedom of conscience, religious freedom, the freedom of each person, each family, each people," he said. "It has been given to you by God himself."[26]

THE THEMATIC JOURNEY

What did Pope Francis really say in America? What did he want Americans—Catholic or not—to learn? He reiterated the same themes that launched his pontificate when he was Cardinal Bergoglio, the same themes that made him the people's pope and the controversial pope.

He wants the Church to "go out." One of the main purposes of the trip was the canonization Mass of St. Junípero Serra. At that Mass, he called Serra "the embodiment of 'a Church which goes forth,' a Church which sets out to bring everywhere the reconciling tenderness of God." He commended Father Serra's motto, which just as well describes Pope Francis's missionary spirit: "*Siempre adelante!* Keep moving forward!"[27]

He is against "economic imperialism." Francis's visit to the United States began with three days in Cuba, giving new life to accusations that Francis is a Marxist sympathizer. John Allen Jr. of the *Boston Globe* argued that, in fact, Pope Francis inserted a "gentle critique of Cuba's Socialist revolution" into his remarks there.[28] On the flight from Cuba to the United States, Gian Guido Vecchi, from the Milan, Italy, daily newspaper *Corriere della Sera*, asked the pope about "sectors of American society which were starting to wonder if the pope was Catholic" and "talk about a 'communist Pope.'"

The pope answered, in part, "I don't believe that I have said anything not found in the Church's social teaching. Things can be explained, and maybe an explanation could give the impression of being a little more 'leftist,' but that would be an error of explanation. No, my teaching, on all of this, in *Laudato Si*, on economic imperialism and all these things, is that of the Church's social teaching. And if I need to recite the Creed, I am ready to do it!"[29]

He is the pope who cares for homosexuals and for morality. By embracing both Yayo Grassi and Kim Davis, Pope Francis shows that no one falls outside the scope of God's love and that no one should suffer discrimination.

He is the peacemaker pope. The keystone of the pope's trip was his address to the United Nations, which was founded to promote peace. However, the emotional highpoint was probably his visit to Ground

Zero in New York. It was one of the few events he mentioned when he spoke briefly at Philadelphia International Airport before leaving. Ground Zero "speaks so powerfully of the mystery of evil," he said. "Yet we know with certainty that evil never has the last word, and that, in God's merciful plan, love and peace triumph over all."[30]

He promotes the right to life and care for mothers. Pope Francis called for the protection of the unborn several times during his trip. For instance, when he listed religious freedom as a "bare minimum" necessity worldwide, he added, "These pillars of integral human development have a common foundation, which is the right to life." At Independence Hall, he echoed St. John Paul II, saying, "The ultimate test of your greatness is the way you treat every human being, but especially the weakest and most defenseless ones."[31]

But my favorite expression of his love for unborn children and their mothers came in Cuba on the day he left for the United States. At a meeting with families, he addressed pregnant women directly. "Right now, put your hands over your baby," he said. "Whether you are here, or following by radio or television, do it now. And to each of them, and to each baby boy or girl you are expecting, I give my blessing.... In the name of the Father, and of the Son, and of the Holy Spirit. And I pray that your child will be born healthy and grow up well, that you can be good parents. Caress the child you are expecting!"

His papacy promotes Christian marriage. Another main purpose of his visit was the World Meeting of Families, where Pope Francis gave a wonderful, impromptu talk in which he spoke of how marriage that is indissoluble, faithful, and open to life is not just a cross but a source of deep happiness. "In families, there are difficulties, but these difficulties are overcome with love," he said. "Hate doesn't overcome any difficulty. Division of hearts doesn't overcome any difficulty. Only love is capable of overcoming difficulties. Love is a festival. Love is joy."[32]

He is the pope who asks us to welcome the stranger. Pope Francis introduced himself at the White House by saying, "As the son of an immigrant family, I am happy to be a guest in this country, which was largely built by such families.[33]

He is the pope who calls us to harmony with nature. Francis vigorously reaffirmed his environmental views once again in America. But he also spoke poignantly about what we lose when we misuse technology. "I would say that at the root of so many contemporary situations is a kind of impoverishment born of a widespread and radical sense of loneliness," he said. "Running after the latest fad, accumulating 'friends' on one of the social networks, we get caught up in what contemporary society has to offer. Loneliness with fear of commitment in a limitless effort to feel recognized."[34]

It is that loneliness that Pope Francis hopes to penetrate with a culture of encounter in the Church. And as is so often the case with him, he demonstrates this best not with words, but by example.

In the end, the most lasting legacy of his visit to the United States wasn't just the words he delivered—it was his very presence, the encounter Americans had with him. And that's what we turn to next.

CHAPTER TEN

Encounters with Francis

"Then the righteous will answer him and say, 'Lord, when did we see
you hungry and feed you, or thirsty and give you drink?'"
—Matthew 25:37

If you want to know what the culture of encounter is, ask John Boehner.
He was the Speaker of the House the day Pope Francis visited the U.S.
Capitol building. The next morning, he announced that he was resigning
from both the speakership and his congressional seat.

If you watch the video or look at the pictures of Pope Francis
addressing Congress, his image is framed by a smiling Joe Biden on
one side and John Boehner on the other, dabbing his face with a hand-
kerchief. Watch the video of Pope Francis blessing the people gathered
outside the Capitol Building and you see the two figures again, only now
John Boehner is openly weeping.

And even that wasn't the worst. "I was really emotional in a moment
where really no one saw," Boehner said in a press conference. "As the
pope and I were getting ready to exit the building we found ourselves
alone. The pope grabbed my left arm and said some very kind words to
me about my commitment to kids and education."

Boehner choked with tears as he told the next part of the story. "Then
the pope puts his arm around me and kind of pulls me toward him and
says, 'Please, pray for me.'"

"Wow," he said, "who am I to pray for the pope? But I did."[1]

Robert Costa, a political reporter at the *Washington Post* said he and
Politico's Jake Sherman ran into the Speaker after the pope's visit and
sensed something was up. Boehner normally brushes past reporters on
his way out of the Capitol at the end of the day, but not this day. He

told and retold his story, repeating the key moments several times in his enthusiasm. Then he stood looking wistfully into the distance before he walked outside.

Boehner's colleagues were stunned to learn at a meeting the next day that Boehner was resigning. Costa wasn't. "If they had seen him Thursday at twilight, vividly remembering a pope's simple request, maybe they wouldn't have been that surprised," he said.[2]

THE POPE FRANCIS EFFECT

There were many reasons for Boehner to want to resign, but Pope Francis was clearly the impetus for the sudden decision. Not the message of Pope Francis—not his words of comfort or challenge—but the very fact of Pope Francis meeting him and taking him seriously as a Christian.

You hear that again and again from people after they meet the pope. Sister Bernadette Rose was a second year novice with the Little Sisters of the Poor in Queens Village, New York, when she traveled to Washington for the canonization Mass of St. Junipero Serra. She told me she was waiting for Mass to begin when her superior got a text message saying that the pope would be visiting their house. The whole group left Mass to be able to greet him. That night at 6:45 PM, police cars and flags filled the street, and Pope Francis arrived in a Fiat.

"He just walked through our chapel doors and there were probably thirty-five sisters ready to greet him," she said. "He made his rounds to every single one of us and took time to talk to us. Each of us. We even have this little Columbian sister who is 102 years old. He asked her if she still likes wine. She said 'No, no, no! Only café.' He smiled and said 'Very good. Me, too.'"

Sister Bernadette said just being with him boosted her faith. "He looked at me and smiled," she said. "I held the hand of the successor of Peter, and his gaze was like Jesus looking into my soul."

The experience left her a little overwhelmed. "I'm still kind of trying to take it in," she said a few days later. "It really affirmed me in my vocation. It really boosts my confidence to live this life of virginity for the Church and for the Lord, which can be difficult."

She said Pope Francis gave the sisters an impromptu speech about the importance of their work with the elderly. "He said our work isn't appreciated, helping the elderly…but that we do it for Jesus. He said every day you need to sing into his ear. Sing, 'I love you Jesus. I'm doing this for you.' Then he said that if it's just one of those days when everything is hard, you can look at that difficult resident and say, 'You know, Jesus, you're really being a nuisance right now. You are really being spoiled, Jesus!' He shook his finger when he said it."

She appreciated the quiet, familiar visit. "When I watched him going into all these crowded, loud atmospheres, taking selfies with teens, meeting kids in Harlem, it really made me appreciate what we had," she said. "Our meeting was just so intimate. That's the word that keeps coming back to me. It was so intimate."[3]

But those who encountered the pope in a crowd had similar experiences of his presence. Ruth Smart of Brooklyn saw him in New York's Central Park and told the Associated Press about it. "As he passed by, you felt a cool, refreshing peace, as if he were spreading a huge blanket of peace through the crowd," she said. "Even though the crowd exploded in a roar, it was pure joy."[4]

Before he arrived, the *New York Times* treated the pope like a traffic story—a terrible storm headed their way. But describing his visit, after the fact, the *Times* dissolved into lyrical joy.

"The layers of political commentary that followed his remarks in Washington earlier in the week seemed to fall away, leaving the day one of pure emotion for Francis and those wishing to be near him," reported the *Times*. It described the scene at the Ground Zero memorial: "There, he paused for a long moment of silent reflection, gazing down into the pool of cascading water, which, from the visitor's vantage point, has no visible bottom."[5]

Julie Rodgers, a seventy-year-old woman, told the *Times*, "I'm Jewish, and this is still the coolest moment of my life."

A Channel 7 reporter in New York interviewed a sobbing woman at Ground Zero after Pope Francis's prayer there. She said she had been present when the twin towers were attacked on September 11, 2001. "I witnessed the atrocities of mankind and I really had lost hope," she said. "I lost faith and I didn't feel that we actually had a chance. And this is the first time ever in the last fourteen years that I actually believe we really do have a chance. It makes that much of a difference." As her sobbing overcame her voice, the interview ended with the reporter hugging her.[6]

The power of the papal presence was described like that, again and again, in coverage of the event: It brought peace, joy—and encouragement. The *National Catholic Register* newspaper asked a number of bishops to sum up their encounters with Pope Francis, and again and again, they summed up the effect of the pope as "encouraging."

"I very much felt his embrace," said Baltimore Archbishop William Lori. "He wanted to show his unity with us as bishops of the United States. That was beautiful and important. He encouraged us to show the same love to fellow priests and engage in a kind of faithful, courageous and creative dialogue with culture and a Church that is a welcoming missionary. I felt very affirmed by that."

"He didn't come in any way, shape or form to chide us," said Bishop Paul Etienne of Cheyenne, Wyoming. "He came to encourage us, to be among us, to tell us not to be afraid. He wants us to be a beacon of light and truth to our people, because they're longing for it."[7]

Francis dealt with non-Catholics the same way, said Father Chris Pollard, who was with the Holy See at the United Nations from 2009 to 2012. "Throughout this whole visit, so far he hasn't taken that tone of correcting people or criticizing people," Father Pollard told Catholic News Agency. "His tone has been using what they already find familiar and agreeable, and trying to take them a few steps closer to the Christian faith."[8]

A CHARISM OF ENCOURAGEMENT

This is Pope Francis's culture of encounter. It begins with his own friendship with Jesus Christ, which comes from his daily routine: Mass, the Breviary, the rosary, and a Eucharistic Hour. Then, he goes out to encounter others, seeing Christ *in* them and bringing Christ *to* them.

This has been the vocation of the pope from the very beginning. The night before he died, Jesus spoke to Peter using his old name. "Simon, Simon, behold Satan has demanded to sift all of you like wheat," he said, "but I have prayed that your own faith may not fail; and once you have turned back, you must strengthen your brothers" (Luke 22:31–32).

You can see this prayer at work in Peter's life in the stories that follow the resurrection of Jesus from the dead. To assure each other of the truth of this event, the Apostles don't just say to each other, "The Lord has risen"—they say, "The Lord has truly been raised and has appeared to Simon!" (Luke 24:34). They don't just have faith and hope—they have faith and hope *with Peter.*

This "charism of encouragement" is by no means a guarantee that the pope will be flawless. In fact, after announcing that he will encourage the others, Peter boasts, "Lord, I am prepared to go to prison and to die with you!" Jesus answers, "I tell you, Peter, before the cock crows this day, you will deny three times that you know me" (Luke 22:33–34).

But despite continued mistakes, Peter's charism shows up in the early Church, as well. In the New Testament, the people behave toward Peter very much like modern-day papal pilgrims. "Thus they even carried the sick out into the streets and laid them on cots and mats so that when Peter came by, at least his shadow might fall on one or another of them," says the book of Acts (5:15).

Peter's shadow had no magical powers, and Peter himself was just a weak fisherman from Galilee who denied Jesus three times. The real power at work in Peter, and in the papacy, is given to them from Jesus Christ. It is a power of attraction that seems to be given a particular intensity in the Vicar of Christ, but can work through any sinner who commits himself to the Lord. People experienced Mother Teresa that way: They felt loved and more loving after they were with her. Or think of the holiest person you have known—a monk or sister or the woman who is always there helping make sandwiches for the needy at the parish. You sense something special in those people. You sense Jesus Christ.

Francis himself explained how this works when he met with bishops in Washington, DC. He didn't speak with the anxious fear of failure that animates so much Catholic discourse in the West. He told the bishops that a shepherd should trust in God enough to leave the important work to him.

"I have not come to judge you or to lecture you," he said. "I trust completely in the voice of the One who 'teaches all things.' Allow me only, in the freedom of love, to speak to you as a brother among brothers."

He told them that staying close to Jesus Christ is their single most important activity. "The heart of our identity is to be sought in constant prayer…not be just any kind of prayer, but familiar union with Christ," he said. "Such trusting union with Christ is what nourishes the life of a pastor."

It is through close familiarity with Jesus that they could discover the simple proclamation of the faith the world needs to hear. "It is not about preaching complicated doctrines, but joyfully proclaiming Christ who died and rose for our sake. The 'style' of our mission should make our hearers feel that the message we preach is meant 'for them.'"

To do this, bishops have to be in constant contact with those they serve. "We are promoters of the culture of encounter," he said. "Dialogue is our method, not as a shrewd strategy but out of fidelity to the One who never wearies of visiting the marketplace, even at the eleventh hour, to propose his offer of love…. I cannot ever tire of encouraging you to dialogue fearlessly."

Pope Francis told the bishops it was vital for them to present the Christian message first not as a critique of the flaws of their listener, but as a lifeline out of their troubles. "Harsh and divisive language does not befit the tongue of a pastor. It has no place in his heart. Although it may momentarily seem to win the day, only the enduring allure of goodness and love remains truly convincing," he said.

A Call to a Culture of Encounter

Pope Francis himself was a model of that pastoral approach again and again during the visit. You can see it in his words to the United Nations staff, who he spoke to apart from his main remarks to the General Assembly. Addressing the "officials and secretaries, translators and interpreters, cleaners and cooks, maintenance and security personnel," he said, "Be close to one another, respect one another, and so embody among yourselves this Organization's ideal of a united human family, living in harmony, working not only *for* peace, but *in* peace; working not only *for* justice, but *in* a spirit of justice."

He followed the same method again and again when addressing various groups of people. First, he deeply respected who they are and what they do. Then he called them to a higher standard. While speaking in Congress, he compared the work of the lawmakers to that of Moses, the great lawmaker in the Old Testament. Then, if they were feeling flattered, he used that image to redefine their vocations, saying, "Moses provides us with a good synthesis of your work: You are asked to protect, by means of the law, the image and likeness fashioned by God on every human face."

In New York, he warned religious: "We can get caught up measuring the value of our apostolic works by the standards of efficiency, good management and outward success which govern the business world." He proposed a better way: "The cross shows us a different way of measuring success. Ours is to plant the seeds: God sees to the fruits of our labors. And if at times our efforts and works seem to fail and produce no fruit, we need to remember that we are followers of Jesus—and his life, humanly speaking, ended in failure, in the failure of the cross."

But perhaps the best articulation of the Francis approach came in his remarks to the lay people attending Mass at Madison Square Garden. He gave them this beautiful summary of the culture of encounter:

> The Gospels tell us how many people came up to Jesus to ask: "Master, what must we do?" The first thing that Jesus does in response is to propose, to encourage, to motivate. He keeps telling his disciples to go, to go out. He urges them to go out and meet others where they really are, not where we think they should be. Go out, again and again, go out without fear, without hesitation. Go out and proclaim this joy which is for all the people.[9]

One sentence by Pope Francis from his remarks to bishops in Philadelphia drives the point home: "A Christianity which 'does' little in practice, while incessantly 'explaining' its teachings, is dangerously unbalanced,"[10] he said. The sentiment brings us back to Pope Francis's preconclave speech and his early pontificate. Christianity is a way of life, not an ideology. He summed up that way of life in Rio de Janeiro when he told young people: "With these two things you have the action plan: the Beatitudes and Matthew 25. You do not need to read anything else."[11]

In the end, the culture of encounter is nothing more than the recollected life of the Beatitudes and the active life of Matthew 25. That is the chapter of Matthew where Jesus tells three stories in which people are rewarded for all eternity or find themselves outside of God's company for all eternity. In each story, it is their sins of omission that damn those who would otherwise have found happiness in the Lord. These stories don't show Jesus rejecting bad people because of the bad things they did. They show him rejecting supposedly good people who didn't go out and encounter those who needed them. In one, a servant buried his talent instead of using it. He got thrown into the darkness outside where there is wailing and grinding of teeth. In another, five foolish virgins didn't keep the oil of active faith replenished in their lamps. So they got shut out of the eternal wedding feast.

In a third story, the great passage on the "Judgment of Nations," Jesus himself separates mankind into two groups. One served the poor; the other didn't. One welcomed the stranger; the other didn't. One visited prisoners; the other didn't. Those who served did so simply and seemingly naturally. They were not looking for a reward. Those who failed to serve didn't reject God or make a decision against their faith; they just never decided to help. The first group goes to heaven; the second doesn't make it. Pope Francis is fond of quoting St. John of the Cross, "In the evening of life, we will be judged on love alone."[12] It is exactly this that he means.

MARY, THE MODEL OF ENCOUNTER

The great model for the culture of encounter is the woman who Francis has kept close to him throughout his pontificate. On his first morning as pope, he went to leave flowers at an image of the Blessed Mother at St. Mary Major in Rome. He visits her image there before every trip. On October 13, seven months into his pontificate, he consecrated the world to her. She is the model he proposed in that first four-minute speech that led to his election as pope, and she is the model he points to at the end of every major papal document.

She is a model of the culture of encounter. She is the one who brings Christ to Elizabeth (Luke 1:41) and to the wedding couple in Cana (John 2:1). She presents Jesus in her lap to the Shepherds and Magi at the beginning of his life, and to the whole world at the foot of the cross. She is the one who gathers the Apostles to wait for Jesus (Acts 1:14), and it is her image that John sees glowing in the sky as the great sign of the Church (Revelation 12:1).

"Whenever we look to Mary," says Pope Francis, "we come to believe once again in the revolutionary nature of love and tenderness."[13]

Ultimately, this is the real revolution Pope Francis wants to start in the Church.

ACKNOWLEDGMENTS

This book would not exist if my wife April wasn't as generous, self-sacrificing, and encouraging as she is (but then neither would a lot of things). I owe thanks to Claudia Volkman, who started the ball rolling, and colleagues at Benedictine College in Atchison, Kansas: Andrew Salzmann, Matthew Ramage, Mark Zia, and, heck, the whole theology floor—who can't be blamed for any theological errors here, but who were very helpful. Thanks also to "devil's advocate" Marc Pecha and the invaluable brain and kindness of Rebecca Teti.

INTRODUCTION

1. Antonio Spadaro, SJ, "A Big Heart Open to God," *America*, September 30, 2013, http://americamagazine.org/pope-interview.

CHAPTER ONE

1. Jimmy Akin. "The 4-Minute Speech That Got Pope Francis Elected?" Catholic Answers Blog. April 23, 2013. www.catholic.com/blog/jimmy-akin/the-4-minute-speech-that-got-pope-francis-elected.
2. Akin.
3. Akin.
4. Manya A. Brachear with Alessandra Maggiorani, "Inside the papal conclave," *Chicago Tribune*, April 21, 2005, http://articles.chicagotribune.com/2005-04-21/news/0504210263_1_papal-conclave-joseph-ratzinger-cardinal-francis-george.
5. Manya A. Brachear, "Cardinal George: Pope Francis Not 'bogged down with a lot of baggage,'" *Chicago Tribune*, March 17, 2013, http://articles.chicagotribune.com/2013-03-17/news/chi-cardinal-george-pope-francis-not-bogged-down-with-a-lot-of-baggage-20130317_1_conclave-cardinal-george-pope-francis.
6. Brachear, "Cardinal George."
7. Cindy Wooden, "Pope Francis Explains Why He Chose St. Francis of Assisi's Name," *Catholic News Service*, March 17, 2013, http://www.catholicnews.com/services/englishnews/2013/pope-francis-explains-why-he-chose-st-francis-of-assisi-s-name.cfm.
8. St. Bonaventure, *The Life of Saint Francis of Assisi*, trans. E. Gurney Saltar (New York: E.P. Dutton, 1904), VI:6. www.ecatholic2000.com/bonaventure/assisi/francis.shtml.
9. St. Bonaventure, "Bonaventure: The Soul's Journey into God, the Tree of Life," in *The Life of St. Francis*, trans. Ewert Cousins (New York: Paulist, 1978), VI:6.
10. Spadaro.
11. Andrea Tornielli, *Francis: Pope of a New World*, trans. William J. Melcher (San Francisco: Ignatius, 2013), chap. 4.
12. Andrea Tornielli, "Pope Francis's First Guide to Catholicism? Grandma Rosa," *La Stampa in English*, March 26, 2013. http://www.lastampa.it/2013/03/26/esteri/lastampa-in-english/pope-francis-first-guide-to-catholicism-grandma-rosa-VYJZAfWGeXXIZjg1QwO4UI/pagina.html.
13 Tornielli, *Francis: Pope of a New World*, 81–82.
14. Tornielli, *Francis: Pope of a New World*, 113–114.
15. "The remembrances of twenty Cardinals," *30 Days*, 4 (2005), www.30giorni.it/articoli_id_8513_l3.htm.
16. Spadaro.

17. Pope Francis, Homily, "Missa Pro Ecclesia" with the Cardinal Electors, Sistine Chapel, March 14, 2013, http://w2.vatican.va/content/francesco/en/homilies/2013/documents/papa-francesco_20130314_omelia-cardinali.html.

18. Pope Francis, Homily, "Missa Pro Ecclesia."

CHAPTER TWO

1. "'This Week' Transcript: Cardinal Timothy Dolan," *ABC News*, March 31, 2013, http://abcnews.go.com/Politics/week-transcript-cardinal-timothy-dolan/story?id=18841802.

2. Pope Francis, Address to the Students of the Jesuit Schools of Italy and Albania, Paul VI Audience Hall, June 7, 2013, https://w2.vatican.va/content/francesco/en/speeches/2013/june/documents/papa-francesco_20130607_scuole-gesuiti.html.

3. "Surprise! New Pope takes a walk through Rome," CatholicCulture.org, April 20, 2005, http://www.catholicculture.org/news/features/index.cfm?recnum=36653.

4. John L. Allen Jr., "Challenges to vision of a 'Poor Church for the Poor,'" *National Catholic Reporter*, March 19, 2013, http://ncronline.org/blogs/ncr-today/challenges-vision-poor-church-poor.

5. Carol Glatz, "Pope washes young offenders' feet at Holy Thursday Mass," *Catholic Herald*, March 28, 2013, http://www.catholicherald.co.uk/news/2013/03/28/pope-washes-young-offenders-feet-at-holy-thursday-mass/.

6. Pope Francis, Homily, Mass of the Lord's Supper, Prison for Minors Casal del Marmo, March 28, 2013, http://w2.vatican.va/content/francesco/en/homilies/2013/documents/papa-francesco_20130328_coena-domini.html.

7. John Allen Jr., "Francis at 100 Days: The world's parish priest," *National Catholic Reporter*, June 17, 2013, http://ncronline.org/news/vatican/francis-100-days-worlds-parish-priest?CFID=37906601&CFTOKEN=50677691&jsessionid=8430baf037e086842b7174465b264069182e.

8. Pope Francis, Chrism Mass Homily, Saint Peter's Basilica, March 28, 2013, http://w2.vatican.va/content/francesco/en/homilies/2013/documents/papa-francesco_20130328_messa-crismale.html.

9. Pope Francis, Chrism Mass Homily.

10. "'This Week' Transcript: Cardinal Timothy Dolan."

11. Pope Francis, Address of Pope Francis to the New Non-Resident Ambassadors to the Holy See, Clementine Hall, May 16, 2013, https://w2.vatican.va/content/francesco/en/speeches/2013/may/documents/papa-francesco_20130516_nuovi-ambasciatori.html.

12. Pope Francis, Address to Ambassadors, March 31, 2013.

13. Pope Francis, Video-Message of Holy Father Francis to Participants in the Initiative Entitled "Ten Squares for Ten Commandments," June 8, 2013, https://w2.vatican.va/content/francesco/en/messages/pont-messages/2013/documents/papa-francesco_20130608_videomessaggio-10piazze.html.

14. *The Baltimore Catechism of 1891* (Boston: The Catholic Primer, 2005), http://www.boston-catholic-journal.com/baltimore_catechism.pdf.

15. Pope Francis, "Laudato Si—Chapter Six: Ecological Education and Spirituality," *Crux*, June 18, 2015, 204, http://www.cruxnow.com/church/2015/06/18/laudato-si-chapter-six-ecological-education-and-spirituality/.

16. Alasdair MacIntyre, "Heedlessness," YouTube video, 1:16:44, Notre Dame Center for Ethics and Culture NDethics, https://youtu.be/ccwTDBMn9Fs.

17. "Towards the End of Poverty," *The Economist*, June 1, 2013. http://www.economist.com/news/leaders/21578665-nearly-1-billion-people-have-been-taken-out-extreme-poverty-20-years-world-should-aim.

18. Pope John Paul II, Message for the World Day of Peace, January 1, 2001, http://w2.vatican.va/content/john-paul-ii/en/messages/peace/documents/hf_jp-ii_mes_20001208_xxxiv-world-day-for-peace.html.

19. Pope Francis, Message for Lent 2016, 3. http://w2.vatican.va/content/francesco/en/messages/lent/documents/papa-francesco_20151004_messaggio-quaresima2016.html.

20. Pope Francis, "Apostolic Exhortation Evangelii Gaudium," EWTN, https://www.ewtn.com/library/PAPALDOC/f1evangaud.HTM.

21. Rush Limbaugh, "It's sad how wrong Pope Francis Is (Unless It's a deliberate Mistranslation by Leftists)," *The Rush Limbaugh Show*, November 27, 2013, http://www.rushlimbaugh.com/daily/2013/11/27/it_s_sad_how_wrong_pope_francis_is_unless_it_s_a_deliberate_mistranslation_by_leftists.

22. Jonathan Freedland, "Why Even Atheists Should Be Praying for Pope Francis," *The Guardian*, November 15, 2013, http://www.theguardian.com/commentisfree/2013/nov/15/atheists-pope-francis-obama-liberal-voice-change.

23. The Editors, "Laudato No: Praise Not Pope Francis's Crude Economics," *National Review*, June 18, 2015, http://www.nationalreview.com/article/420013/laudato-no-praise-not-pope-franciss-crude-economics-editors?target=author&tid=900569.

24. Maureen Mullarkey, "Where Did Pope Francis's Extravagant Rant Come From?" *The Federalist*, June 24, 2015, http://thefederalist.com/2015/06/24/where-did-pope-franciss-extravagant-rant-come-from/.

25. David Brooks, "Fracking and the Franciscans," *The New York Times*, June 23, 2015, http://www.nytimes.com/2015/06/23/opinion/fracking-and-the-franciscans.html?_r=1.

26. Pope Francis, "Laudato Si—Chapter Three: The Human Roots of the Ecological Crisis," *Crux*, June 18, 2015, 129, http://www.cruxnow.com/church/2015/06/18/laudato-si-chapter-three-the-human-roots-of-the-ecological-crisis/.

27. Pope John Paul II, *Centesimus Annus*, 49.

28. Pope Francis, "Laudato Si—Chapter Five: Lines of Action and Approach," *Crux*, June 18, 2015, 198. http://www.cruxnow.com/church/2015/06/18/laudato-si-chapter-five-lines-of-approach-and-action/.

29. Pope Francis, *Laudato Sí*, 144.

30. Alasdair MacIntyre, "Heedlessness."

31. Pope Francis, *Laudato Sí*, 129.

32. Pope Francis, *Laudato Sí*, 129.

33. William Baumol, Robert Litan, and Carl Schramm, *Good Capitalism/Bad Capitalism* (New Haven, CT: Yale University Press, 2007), 30.

34. Many examples of this "parable" can be found in business books and in talks and homilies online. I wish I knew who originated the story.

35. Pope Francis, *Lumen Fidei*, 13.

Chapter Three

1. Annie Thompson and Henry Ausin, "Pope: 'Who am I to judge' gay people?" *NBC News*, July 29, 2013, http://www.nbcnews.com/news/other/pope-who-am-i-judge-gay-people-f6C10780741.

2. Spadaro.

3. Spadaro.

4. Pope Francis, *Evangelii Gaudium*, 64.

5. "Full Text: Pope Francis's opening Address to Humanum conference," *Catholic Herald*, November 17, 2014, http://www.catholicherald.co.uk/news/2014/11/17/full-text-pope-franciss-opening-address-to-humanum-conference/.

6. Pope Francis, Address to the Bishops of the Episcopal Conference of South Africa on Their "Ad Limina" Visit, April 25, 2014, https://w2.vatican.va/content/francesco/en/speeches/2014/april/documents/papa-francesco_20140425_ad-limina-africa.html.

7. Elisabeth Piqué, "The Synod on the Family: 'The divorced and remarried seem excommunicated,'" *La Nacion*, December 7, 2014, http://www.lanacion.com.ar/1750351-the-synod-on-the-family-the-divorced-and-remarried-seem-excommunicated.

8. Rachel Weiner, "How Hillary Clinton evolved on gay marriage," *Washington Post*, March 18, 2013, https://www.washingtonpost.com/news/the-fix/wp/2013/03/18/how-hillary-clinton-evolved-on-gay-marriage/.

9. Lucy Shackelford and Madonna Lebling, "Timeline of Obama's Gay Marriage Views," *Washington Post*, May 9, 2012, https://www.washingtonpost.com/politics/timeline-of-obamas-gay-marriage-views/2012/05/09/gIQArlQPEU_story.html.

10. Anthony Fisher, "Same Sex Marriage Undermines Purpose of the Institution," *The Australian*, May 30, 2015, http://www.theaustralian.com.au/opinion/samesex-marriage-undermines-purpose-of-the-institution/news-story/8e5231504c205c3a217ff1d702dd651a.

11. Pope Francis, "Full Text of Pope's In-Flight Interview from Manila to Rome," Catholic News Agency. January 19, 2015, http://www.catholicnewsagency.com/news/full-text-of-popes-in-flight-interview-from-manila-to-rome-84716/.

12. Pope Francis, *Amoris Laetitia*, 11.

13. Pope Francis, *The Name of God Is Mercy, a Conversation with Andrew Tornielli*, trans. Oonagh Stransky (New York: Random House, 2015), 62.

14. Pope Francis, Address to participants in the ecclesial convention of the Diocese of Rome, Paul VI Audience Hall, June 17, 2013, https://w2.vatican.va/content/francesco/en/speeches/2013/june/documents/papa-francesco_20130617_convegno-diocesano-roma.html.

15. Pope Francis, Meeting with Young People, Kololo Air Strip, Kampala (Uganda), November 28, 2015, https://w2.vatican.va/content/francesco/en/speeches/2015/november/documents/papa-francesco_20151128_uganda-giovani.html.

16. Scott James, "Many Successful Gay Marriages Share an Open Secret," *The New York Times*, January 28, 2010, http://www.nytimes.com/2010/01/29/us/29sfmetro.html.

17. Nico Lang, "Gay Open Marriages Need to Come Out of the Closet," *The Daily Beast*, December 31, 2015, http://www.thedailybeast.com/articles/2016/01/01/gay-open-marriages-need-to-come-out-of-the-closet.html.

18. Elise Harris, "'What is being proposed is not marriage'— Pope Calls for Defense of Family," Catholic News Agency, October 26, 2014, http://www.catholicnewsagency.com/news/what-is-being-proposed-is-not-marriage-pope-calls-for-defense-of-family-12766/.

19. "Gay Voices Against Gay Marriage: Jean Pier," NOM Blog, January 10, 2013, http://www.nomblog.com/32272/.

20. Tom Hoopes, "Can Gay Marriage Be Stopped?" *Crisis Magazine*, July 1, 2002, http://www.crisismagazine.com/2002/can-same-sex-marriage-be-stopped.

21. Pope Francis, In-flight Press Conference from the Philippines to Rome, January 19, 2015, http://w2.vatican.va/content/francesco/en/speeches/2015/january/documents/papa-francesco_20150119_srilanka-filippine-conferenza-stampa.html.

22. Rosie Scammell, "Children need heterosexual parents, says pope after gay pride march," *Religion News Service*, June 15, 2015, http://www.religionnews.com/2015/06/15/children-need-heterosexual-parents-says-pope-after-gay-pride-march/.

23. Pope Francis, *Amoris Laetitia*, 52, 56.

24. Elisabeth Piqué, "The Synod on the Family."

25. Austen Ivereigh, *The Great Reformer: Francis and the Making of a Radical Pope* (New York: Henry Holt and Company), 140–141.

CHAPTER FOUR

1. Bishop James Conley, "A World Youth Day—and a Pope—of Surprises," *National Catholic Register* blog, July 29, 2013, http://www.ncregister.com/blog/wyd-witnesses/a-world-youth-day-and-a-pope-of-surprises.

2. "Pope Cries with Brazilian Child Who Wants to Be a Priest," Catholic News Agency, July 31, 2013, http://www.ncregister.com/daily-news/pope-cries-with-brazilian-child-who-wants-to-be-a-priest/.

3. Jeanette de Melo, "Way of the Cross, a Most Intense Moment, Says Pope" *National Catholic Register* blog, July 27, 2013, http://www.ncregister.com/blog/wyd-witnesses/way-of-the-cross-a-most-intense-moment-says-pope.

4. "World Youth Day Testimonies," Presentation of the Blessed Virgin Mary Parish, Jamaica, New York, http://www.presentationbvmjamaica.org/web/index.php/news-a-events/world-youth-day-testimonies.

5. "World Youth Day Testimonies."

6. Pope Francis, Prayer Vigil with the Young People, Waterfront of Copacabana, Rio de Janeiro, July 27, 2013, https://w2.vatican.va/content/francesco/en/speeches/2013/july/documents/papa-francesco_20130727_gmg-veglia-giovani.html.

7. Pope Francis, Homily, Holy Mass on the Occasion of the XXVIII World Youth Day, Waterfront of Copacabana, Rio de Janeiro, July 28, 2013, http://w2.vatican.va/content/francesco/en/homilies/2013/documents/papa-francesco_20130728_celebrazione-xxviii-gmg.html.

8. Tom Hoopes, "Lector for Rio's Millions Met Christ," *The Gregorian* (blog), August 2, 2013, http://www.thegregorian.org/blog/lector-for-rios-millions-met-christ.

9. Estefania Aguirre, "Pope's Vigil for Syrian Peace Expected to Be Biggest in Decades," Catholic News Agency, September 5, 2013, http://www.catholicnewsagency.com/news/popes-vigil-for-syrian-peace-expected-to-be-biggest-in-decades/.

10. Ben Hubbard and Hwaida Saad, "Images of Death in Syria, but No Proof of Chemical Attack," *New York Times*, August 21, 2013, http://www.nytimes.com/2013/08/22/world/middleeast/syria.html.

11. Joby Warrick, "More Than 1,400 killed in Syrian Chemical Weapons Attack, U.S. Says," *The Washington Post*, August 30, 2013, https://www.washingtonpost.com/world/national-security/nearly-1500-killed-in-syrian-chemical-weapons-attack-us-says/2013/08/30/b2864662-1196-11e3-85b6-d27422650fd5_story.html.

12. Pope Francis, *Angelus*, Saint Peter's Square, September, 1, 2013, https://w2.vatican.va/content/francesco/en/angelus/2013/documents/papa-francesco_angelus_20130901.html.

13. Kerri Lenartowick, "Tourists and Pilgrims Pray for Peace at Vatican Vigil," Catholic News Agency, Sept. 7, 2013, http://www.catholicnewsagency.com/

news/tourists-and-pilgrims-pray-for-peace-at-vatican-vigil/.

14. Lenartowick.

15. Pope Francis, Vigil of Prayer for Peace, Saint Peter's Square, September 7, 2013, http://w2.vatican.va/content/francesco/en/homilies/2013/documents/papa-francesco_20130907_veglia-pace.html.

16. Lenartowick.

17. Pope Francis, In-flight press conference from Korea to Rome, August 18, 2014, http://w2.vatican.va/content/francesco/en/speeches/2014/august/documents/papa-francesco_20140818_corea-conferenza-stampa.html.

18. Pope Francis, In-flight press conference from Korea to Rome.

19. Brennan Pursell, *Benedict of Bavaria* (North Haven: Circle, 2008).

20. Pope Francis, *Angelus*, Saint Peter's Square, September 14, 2014, http://w2.vatican.va/content/francesco/en/angelus/2014/documents/papa-francesco_angelus_20140914.html.

21. Pope Francis, *Angelus*, Castel Gandolfo, July 14, 2013, http://w2.vatican.va/content/francesco/en/angelus/2013/documents/papa-francesco_angelus_20130714.html.

22. Pope Francis, Interreligious meeting, Address at Ground Zero Memorial, New York, September 25, 2015, http://w2.vatican.va/content/francesco/en/speeches/2015/september/documents/papa-francesco_20150925_usa-ground-zero.html.

23. Nello Scavo, *Bergoglio's List: How a Young Francis Defied a Dictatorship and Saved Dozens of Lives*, (Charlotte, NC: Saint Benedict Press, 2014), 143.

24. Scavo, preface.

25. Scavo.

26. John Lewis Gaddis, *The Cold War: A New History* (New York: Penguin, 2005), 116–117.

27. Stephen Bates, "Devout Poles show Britain how to keep the faith," *The Guardian*, December 22, 2006, http://www.theguardian.com/uk/2006/dec/23/religion.anglicanism.

28. "Pope Francis Prays for Comfort, Peace at Ground Zero," *National Catholic Register*, September 25, 2015, http://m.ncregister.com/46697/d#.VrPb0tIrLIU.

29. "Pope Francis Prays for Comfort, Peace at Ground Zero"

30. "Pope Francis Prays for Comfort, Peace at Ground Zero."

CHAPTER FIVE

1. Carol Glatz, "Pope Phones People All the Time, Says Vatican official," *UK Catholic Herald*, September 16, 2013, http://www.catholicherald.co.uk/news/2013/09/16/pope-phones-people-all-the-time-says-vatican-official/.

2. Elisabetta Povoledo and Dan Bilefsky, "The pope Gets on the Line, and Everyone Is Talking," *The New York Times*, September 9, 2013, http://www.nytimes.com/2013/09/10/world/europe/the-popes-on-the-line-and-everyones-talking.html?_r=0.

3. Alessandro Speciale and David Gibson, "Pope Francis, the 'cold-call pope,' Reaches Out and Touches a Lot of People," *Washington Post*, September 6, 2013, https://www.washingtonpost.com/national/on-faith/pope-francis-the-cold-call-pope-reaches-out-and-touches-a-lot-of-people/2013/09/06/2f3c3db4-1724-11e3-961c-f22d3aaf19ab_story.html.

4. Speciale and Gibson, "Pope Francis, the 'cold-call pope.'"

5. Pope Francis, Address to participants in the meeting organized by the international federal of Catholic medical associations, Clementine Hall, September 20, 2013, http://w2.vatican.va/content/francesco/en/speeches/2013/september/documents/papa-francesco_20130920_associazioni-medici-cattolici.html.

6. Antonio Spadaro, "Interview with Pope Francis," September 2013, https://w2.vatican.va/content/francesco/en/speeches/2013/september/documents/papa-francesco_20130921_intervista-spadaro.html.

7. Spadaro.

8. Pope Benedict XVI, Interview in preparation for the upcoming journey to Bavaria, Apostolic Palace of Castel Gandolfo, August 5, 2006, http://w2.vatican.va/content/benedict-xvi/en/speeches/2006/august/documents/hf_ben-xvi_spe_20060805_intervista.html.

9. Pope Benedict, Address to the Bishops of Switzerland, November 9, 2006, http://w2.vatican.va/content/benedict-xvi/en/speeches/2006/november/documents/hf_ben-xvi_spe_20061109_concl-swiss-b.

10. Spadaro.

11. Spadaro.

12. Pope Francis, "Faith Is Not Casuistry," Chapel of the Domus Sanctae Marthae, February 21, 2014, https://w2.vatican.va/content/francesco/en/cotidie/2014/documents/papa-francesco-cotidie_20140221_faith-not-casuistry.html.

13. Pope Francis, "Faith Is Not Casuistry."

14. Pope Francis, Address to bishops of South Africa on their "Ad limina" visit, April 25, 2014, http://m2.vatican.va/content/francesco/en/speeches/2014/april/documents/papa-francesco_20140425_ad-limina-africa.html.

15. Pope Francis, Letter according to which an indulgence is granted, September 1, 2015, https://w2.vatican.va/content/francesco/en/letters/2015/documents/papa-francesco_20150901_lettera-indulgenza-giubileo-misericordia.html.

16. Lydia Saad, "Americans Choose 'Pro-Choice' for First Time in Seven Years," *Gallup*, May 29, 2015, http://www.gallup.com/poll/183434/americans-choose-pro-choice-first-time-seven-years.aspx.

17. *General Conference of the Bishops of Latin America and the Caribbean: Concluding Document*, Aparecida, May 31, 2007, 436, http://www.aecrc.org/documents/Aparecida-Concluding%20Document.pdf.

18. Cardinal Joseph Ratzinger, "Worthiness to Receive Holy Communion: General Principals," July, 2004, http://www.ewtn.com/library/CURIA/

cdfworthycom.HTM.

19. Thomas J. Craughwell: *Pope Francis: The Pope from the End of the Earth* (Charlotte, NC: Saint Benedict, 2013), 111–112.

20. Czarina Ong, "Pope Calls Rome Mayor a 'Pretend Catholic' Who Supports Gay Marriage and Euthanasia," *Christian Today*, September 30, 2015, http://www.christiantoday.com/article/pope.calls.rome.mayor.a.pretend.catholic.who.supports.gay.marriage.and.euthanasia/66166.htm.

21. Pope Francis, *Evangelii Gaudium*, 213.

22. Pope Francis, Address to Members of the diplomatic corps accredited to the Holy See, Sala Regia, January 13, 2014, http://w2.vatican.va/content/francesco/en/speeches/2014/january/documents/papa-francesco_20140113_corpo-diplomatico.html.

23. Noted by Gerald O'Connor, "Pope Francis: 'I Have Not Watched Television Since 1990,'" *America*, May 25, 2015, http://americamagazine.org/content/dispatches/pope-francis-i-have-not-watched-television-1990.

24. Pope Francis, Address to a Delegation from the Dignitatis Humanae Institute, Clementine Hall, December 7, 2013, http://w2.vatican.va/content/francesco/en/speeches/2013/december/documents/papa-francesco_20131207_istituto-dignitatis.html.

25. Pope Francis, "Today's World Demands a Common Witness," *L'Osservatore Romano*, October 31, 2013, http://www.osservatoreromano.va/en/news/todays-world-demands-a-common-witness.

26. Pope Francis, *The Name of God Is Mercy*, 60–61.

CHAPTER SIX

1. Mark Binelli, "Pope Francis: The Times They Are A-Changin'," *Rolling Stone*, January 28, 2014, http://www.rollingstone.com/culture/news/pope-francis-the-times-they-are-a-changin-20140128.

2. Howard Chua-Eoan and Elizabeth Dias, "Pope Francis, The People's Pope," *Time*, December 11, 2013, http://poy.time.com/2013/12/11/person-of-the-year-pope-francis-the-peoples-pope/.

3. Nancy Gibbs, "Pope Francis, The Choice," *Time*, December 11, 2013, http://poy.time.com/2013/12/11/pope-francis-the-choice/.

4. Sacred Congregation of the Discipline of the Sacraments, *Quam Singulari*, Decree on First Communion, 1910, http://www.ewtn.com/library/CURIA/CDWFIRST.htm.

5. Pope St. Pius X, *Sacra Tridentina*, "On Frequent and Daily Reception of Holy Communion," December 20, 1905, https://www.ewtn.com/library/CURIA/CDWFREQ.HTM

6. Pope Francis, *Angelus*, Saint Peter's Square, August 16, 2015, https://w2.vatican.va/content/francesco/en/angelus/2015/documents/papa-francesco_angelus_20150816.html.

7. Pope John Paul II, *Ecclesia de Eucharistia*, 2003, 26, http://www. vatican.va/holy_father/special_features/encyclicals/documents/ hf_jp-ii_enc_20030417_ecclesia_eucharistia_en.html.

8. General Conference of the Bishops of Latin America and the Caribbean, 177.

9. United States Conference of Catholic Bishops, "Happy Are Those Who Are Called to His Supper," *On Preparing to Receive Christ Worthily in the Eucharist*, November 14, 2006, http://www.usccb.org/about/doctrine/publications/ upload/statement-happy-are-those-who-are-called-to-his-supper-2006-11-14. pdf.

10. Pope Francis, *Amoris Laetitia*, 12.

11. Pope Francis, *Amoris Laetitia*, 123.

12. As quoted by Pope Francis, *Amoris Laetitia*, 124.

13. Pope Francis, *Amoris Laetitia*, 241.

14. Elise Harris, "Catholic Divorce 'Doesn't Exist,' Pope Francis Says on Return Flight from U.S." *National Catholic Register*, September 28, 2015, http://www.ncregister.com/daily-news/ catholic-divorce-doesnt-exist-pope-francis-says-on-return-flight-from-us/.

15. Pope Francis, In-flight press conference from Korea to Rome, August 18, 2014, https://w2.vatican.va/content/francesco/en/speeches/2014/august/documents/ papa-francesco_20140818_corea-conferenza-stampa.html.

16. Pope Francis, *The Name of God Is Mercy*.

17. "Pope Francis Off the Cuff: The Family Is a Living Symbol of the Loving Plan of God," *National Catholic Register*, September 26, 2015, http://www.ncregister.com/daily-news/ pope-the-family-is-the-living-symbol-of-the-loving-plan-of-god

18. Pope Francis, "Three Loves for One Wedding," June 2, 2014, http://m.vatican. va/content/francescomobile/en/cotidie/2014/documents/papa-francesco- cotidie_20140602_three-loves.html.

19. Pope Francis, Address to engaged couples preparing for marriage, Saint Peter's Square, February 14, 2014, https://w2.vatican.va/content/francesco/ en/speeches/2014/february/documents/papa-francesco_20140214_incontro- fidanzati.html.

20. Andrea Gagliarducci, "Cardinal Kasper's Speech on Divorce, Remarriage and Communion," *National Catholic Register*, March 4, 2014, http://www.ncregister.com/daily-news/ cardinal-kaspers-speech-on-divorce-remarriage-and-communion/.

21. Dennis Coday and Joshua J. McElwee, "Francis Preaches Mercy, Forgiveness on First Papal Sunday," *National Catholic Reporter*, March 17, 2013, http://ncronline.org/news/vatican/ francis-preaches-mercy-forgiveness-first-papal-sunday.

22. Synod of Bishops, *Instrumentum Laboris*, The Pastoral Challenges of the Family in the Context of Evangelization, 2014, http://www.vatican.va/roman_curia/synod/documents/

rc_synod_doc_20140626_instrumentum-laboris-familia_en.html.

23. John Burger, "In New Interview, Pope Francis Defends Decision on Cardinal Burke," *Aleteia*, December 9, 2014, http://aleteia.org/2014/12/09/in-new-interview-pope-francis-defends-decision-on-cardinal-burke/.

24. George Weigel, "Light from the South," *First Things*, June 13, 2012, http://www.firstthings.com/web-exclusives/2012/06/light-from-the-south.

25. Austen Ivereigh, *The Great Reformer: Francis and the Making of a Radical Pope* (New York: Henry Holt), 298.

26. Pope Francis, *Amoris Laetitia*, 62.

27. Pope Francis, *Amoris Laetitia*, 296.

28. Pope Francis, *Amoris Laetitia*, 53.

29. Pope Francis, *Amoris Laetitia*, 298.

30. Fr. Dwight Longenecker, "The Pope's Exhortation—A Parish Priest's Perspective," Patheos, *Standing on My Head* (blog), April 9, 2016, http://www.patheos.com/blogs/standingonmyhead/2016/04/the-popes-exhortation-a-parish-priests-perspective.html.

31. Pope Francis, *Amoris Laetitia*, 301.

32. Ivereigh, *The Great Reformer*, 326.

CHAPTER SEVEN

1. Inés San Martín, "Tattoos aren't just a fashion statement for Egypt's Copts," *Crux*, June 27, 2015, http://www.cruxnow.com/faith/2015/06/27/tattoos-arent-just-a-fashion-statement-for-egypts-copts/.

2. Sarah Pulliam Bailey, "Pope Francis denounces ISIS beheadings: 'Their blood confesses Christ'" *The Washington Post*, February 16, 2015, https://www.washingtonpost.com/news/local/wp/2015/02/16/pope-francis-denounces-isis-beheadings-their-blood-confesses-christ/.

3. Sophia Jones, "ISIS Boasted of These Christians' Deaths. Here Are the Lives They Lived," *The World Post*, updated March 27, 2015, http://www.huffingtonpost.com/2015/02/18/isis-christians-killed-_n_6703278.html?utm_hp_ref=tw.

4. The widely published freelance photojournalist Jonathan Rashad posted stories about the Coptic martyrs at both Vice News on February 26, 2015, and The Islamic Monthly on March 4, 2015, https://news.vice.com/article/christian-martyrs-change-the-world-we-meet-the-families-of-the-egyptian-christians-beheaded-by-the-islamic-state http://theislamicmonthly.com/21-egyptians-beheaded-by-isis.

5. Stefan J. Bos, "African Man Turns to Christ Moments Before Beheading," *BosNewsLife*, April 23, 2015, http://www.bosnewslife.com/35141-african-man-turns-to-christ-moments-before-beheading#comments.

6. Ian Lee and Jethro Mullen, "After ISIS slaughters Christians, an Egyptian village mourns its sons," CNN, February 19, 2015, http://www.cnn.com/2015/02/18/middleeast/egypt-christians-grieving-village/.

7. Pope Francis, In-flight press conference from Istanbul to Rome, November 30, 2014, http://w2.vatican.va/content/francesco/en/speeches/2014/november/documents/papa-francesco_20141130_turchia-conferenza-stampa.html.

8. Pope Francis, General Audience, Saint Peter's Square, June 19, 2013, http://w2.vatican.va/content/francesco/en/audiences/2013/documents/papa-francesco_20130619_udienza-generale.html.

9. Pope Francis, General Audience, Saint Peter's Square, June 19, 2013.

10. Pope John Paul II, *Ut Unum Sint*, 1995, 95, http://w2.vatican.va/content/john-paul-ii/en/encyclicals/documents/hf_jp-ii_enc_25051995_ut-unum-sint.html.

11. Pope Francis, In-flight press conference from Istanbul to Rome, November 30, 2014.

12. Congregation for the Doctrine of the Faith, *Dominus Iesus*, 2000, 17, http://www.vatican.va/roman_curia/congregations/cfaith/documents/rc_con_cfaith_doc_20000806_dominus-iesus_en.html.

13. Edward Pentin, "Pope Tells Lutheran to 'Talk to the Lord' about Receiving the Eucharist," *National Catholic Register*, November 16, 2015, http://www.ncregister.com/blog/edward-pentin/pope-tells-lutheran-to-talk-to-the-lord-about-receiving-eucharist.

14. Allowance of Eucharistic communion for Protestants in rare, extreme circumstances is found in the Code of Canon Law, Canon 844 §4, http://www.vatican.va/archive/ENG1104/_P2T.HTM.

15. Edward Pentin, "Finnish Catholic Spokesman: Communion for Lutherans at the Vatican Was a Mistake," *National Catholic Register*, January 28, 2016, http://www.ncregister.com/blog/edward-pentin/finnish-catholic-spokesman-communion-for-lutherans-at-the-vatican-was-a-mis.

16. Pope Francis, General Audience, Saint Peter's Square, May 15, 2013, http://w2.vatican.va/content/francesco/en/audiences/2013/documents/papa-francesco_20130515_udienza-generale.html.

17. Congregation for the Doctrine of the Faith, *Dominus Iesus*, 4.

18. Brad S. Gregory, "The Unintended Reformation: How a Religious Revolution Secularized Society" (Cambridge and London: The Belknap Press of Harvard University Press, 2012), 111.

19. Pope Francis, *Lumen Fidei*, 35.

20. Pope Francis, In-flight press conference from Istanbul to Rome, November 30, 2014.

21. Ed West, "A Modern Christian Martyr Fr. Ragheed Ganni, Iraqi Christians," Kaldaya.net, June 3, 2009, http://www.kaldaya.net/2009/06/June04_09_E2_FrRagheedGanni_ChristianMartyr.html.

22. "Ragheed, a 'Costly Sacrifice' so that Iraq May See the Dawn of Reconciliation, Says Pope," *Asia News*, June 4, 2007, http://www.asianews.it/index.php?l=en&art=9452&geo=&theme=&size=A.

23. CIA World Factbook, "Middle East: Iraq," https://www.cia.gov/library/publications/the-world-factbook/geos/iz.html.

24. Religious Freedom Report, *Iraq*, http://religion-freedom-report.org.uk/wp-content/uploads/country-reports/iraq.pdf.

25. Janin di Giovanni and Conor Gaffey, "The New Exodus: Christians Flee ISIS in the Middle East," *Newsweek*, March 26, 2015, http://www.newsweek.com/2015/04/03/new-exodus-christians-flee-isis-middle-east-316785.html.

26. European Parliament, "Motion for a Resolution," October 3, 2015, http://www.europarl.europa.eu/sides/getDoc.do?type=MOTION&reference=B8-2015-0256&language=EN.

27. Rick Gladstone, "Syria: U.N. Notes 'Shameful Milestone,'" *The New York Times*, August 23, 2013, http://www.nytimes.com/2013/08/24/world/middleeast/syria-un-notes-shameful-milestone.html.

28. Dave Gibson, "Pope Francis: 'Jesus was popular and look how that turned out,'" *Religion News Service*, September 14, 2015, http://www.religionnews.com/2015/09/14/pope-francis-jesus-popular-time-look-turned/.

29. Anthony Faiola and Michael Birnbaum, "Pope calls on Europe's Catholics to take in refugees," *The Washington Post*, September 6, 2015, https://www.washingtonpost.com/world/refugees-keep-streaming-into-europe-as-crisis-continues-unabated/2015/09/06/8a330572-5345-11e5-b225-90edbd49f362_story.html.

30. Dave Gibson, "Pope Francis."

31. Pope Francis, Message for the World Day of Migrants and Refugees, August 5, 2013, http://w2.vatican.va/content/francesco/en/messages/migration/documents/papa-francesco_20130805_world-migrants-day.html.

32. James Pasto, "Italian immigrants and violent crime," Bostoniano, January 22, 2014, http://bostoniano.info/northendspirit/italian-immigrants-violent-crime/.

33. Carolyn Moehling and Anne Morrison Piehl, "Immigration, Crime and Incarceration in Early Twentieth-Century America," *Demography*, 46(4): 739–763, http://www.ncbi.nlm.nih.gov/pmc/articles/PMC2831353.

34. Encyclopedia Britannica Online, s.v. "American Protective Association (APA)," http://www.britannica.com/topic/American-Protective-Association.

35. Roland G. Fryer Jr. and Steven D. Levitt, "Hatred and Profits: Under the Hood of the Ku Klux Klan,*" *Quarterly Journal of Economics* (2012), 1883–1884.

36. Jim Yardley, "Pope Francis Takes 12 Refugees Back to the Vatican After Trip to Greece," *The New York Times*, April 16, 2016, http://www.nytimes.com/2016/04/17/world/europe/pope-francis-visits-lesbos-heart-of-europes-refugee-crisis.html?_r=0.

37. Pope Francis, Meeting with the Bishops of the United States of America, Cathedral of Saint Matthew, Washington, D.C., September 23, 2015, https://w2.vatican.va/content/francesco/en/speeches/2015/september/documents/papa-francesco_20150923_usa-vescovi.html.

38. Jonathan Rashad, "IN PICTURES: Relatives of Egyptian Christians Killed by IS Speak Out," Middle East Eye,

February 21, 2015, http://www.middleeasteye.net/news/
pictures-relatives-egyptian-christians-killed-speak-out-1637676770.

CHAPTER EIGHT

1. Art Swift, "Pope Francis' Favorable Rating Drops in U.S.," Gallup, July 22, 2015, http://www.gallup.com/poll/184283/pope-francis-favorable-rating-drops.aspx.

2. Austen Ivereigh, *The Great Reformer: Francis and the Making of a Radical Pope* (New York: Henry Holt and Company, 2014), 257–260; 262–263; 355.

3. Andrea Gagliarducci, "Are an Atheist Journalist's Papal Interviews Reliable?" Catholic News Agency, October 29, 2014, http://www.catholicnewsagency.com/news/are-an-atheist-journalists-papal-interviews-reliable-75535/.

4. Andrea Gagliarducci, "Scalfari Confesses: Pope's Words in Interview May Not Have Been His Own," *National Catholic Register*, November 22, 2013, https://www.ncregister.com/daily-news/scalfari-confesses-popes-words-in-interview-may-not-have-been-his-own/.

5. Eugenio Scalfari, "Interview with Pope Francis by the Founder of Italian Daily 'La Repubblica,'" October 9, 2013, http://www.vatican-stg.va/content/francesco/en/speeches/2013/october/documents/papa-francesco_20131002_intervista-scalfari.html.

6. Edward Pentin, "Fr. Lombardi: Latest Scalfari Article on Pope 'In No Way Reliable,'" *National Catholic Register*, November 2, 2015, http://www.ncregister.com/blog/edward-pentin/fr.-lombardi-latest-scalfari-article-on-pope-in-no-way-reliable.

7. Pope Francis, Address on the occasion of the Inauguration of the Bust in Honor of Pope Benedict, Casina of Pius IV, October 27, 2014, https://w2.vatican.va/content/francesco/en/speeches/2014/october/documents/papa-francesco_20141027_plenaria-accademia-scienze.html.

8. Rick Gladstone, "Dogs in Heaven? Pope Francis Leaves Pearly Gates Open," *The New York Times*, December 11, 2014, http://www.nytimes.com/2014/12/12/world/europe/dogs-in-heaven-pope-leaves-pearly-gate-open-.html?_r=0.

9. "Transcript: Pope Francis' March 5 Interview with Corriere della Sera," Catholic News Agency, March 5, 2014, http://www.catholicnewsagency.com/news/transcript-pope-francis-march-5-interview-with-corriere-della-sera/.

10. "Transcript: Pope Francis' March 5 Interview."

11. Pope Francis, Meeting with Families, Mall of Asia Arena, Manila, January 6, 2015, http://w2.vatican.va/content/francesco/en/speeches/2015/january/documents/papa-francesco_20150116_srilanka-filippine-incontro-famiglie.html.

12. Mary Eberstadt, *Adam and Eve After the Pill: Paradoxes of the Sexual Revolution* (San Francisco: Ignatius, 2012); and Janet Smith, "Pope Paul VI as Prophet: Have Humane Vitae's Bold predictions come true?'" University of Dallas,

https://www3.nd.edu/~afreddos/courses/264/popepaul.htm.

13. Margery Eagan, "Feeling devastated by this pope," *Crux*,
January 17, 2015, http://www.cruxnow.com/faith/2015/01/17/
feeling-devastated-by-this-pope/?s_campaign=crux:email:onsp.

14. Joseph Brean, "'I felt a hypocrite': Author Michael Coren on Why He Left the
Catholic Church for Anglicanism," *National Post*, May 1, 2015, http://news.
nationalpost.com/news/religion/i-felt-a-hypocrite-author-michael-coren-on-
why-he-left-the-catholic-church-for-anglicanism.

15. Pope Francis, In-flight Press Conference from the Philippines to Rome,
January 19, 2015.

16. Pope Francis, General Audience, Paul VI Audience Hall, January 21, 2015,
http://w2.vatican.va/content/francesco/en/audiences/2015/documents/papa-
francesco_20150121_udienza-generale.html.

17. Pope Francis, General Audience, February 11, 2015, http://w2.vatican.va/
content/francesco/en/audiences/2015/documents/papa-francesco_20150211_
udienza-generale.html.

18. See Pope Francis, *Amoris Laetitia*, 82.

19. "The Pope on His Return Flight to Rome: Encourage Latin America's
Young Church," July 14, 2015, http://www.news.va/en/news/
the-pope-on-his-return-flight-to-rome-encourage-la.

20. Dennis Prager, "Why Pope Francis Is Keeping His
Hammer-and-Sickle Crucifix," *National Review*, July 14,
2015, http://www.nationalreview.com/article/421133/
why-pope-francis-keeping-his-hammer-and-sickle-crucifix-dennis-prager.

21. Erasmo Leiva-Merikakis, *Fire of Mercy, Heart of the Word: Meditations on the
Gospel According to Matthew* (San Francisco: Ignatius, 1996), 186.

22. Pope Francis, *Laudato Sí*, 76.

23. Pope Francis, *Laudato Sí*, 12.

24. Pope Francis, *Laudato Sí*, 202.

25. Pope Francis, *Laudato Sí*, 120.

26. Pope Francis, *Laudato Sí*, 155.

27. Pope Francis, *Laudato Sí*, 225.

28. George F. Will, "Pope Francis's fact-free flamboyance," *The Washington Post*,
September 18, 2015, https://www.washingtonpost.com/opinions/pope-
franciss-fact-free-flamboyance/2015/09/18/7d711750-5d6a-11e5-8e9e-
dce8a2a2a679_story.html.

29. Damon Linker, "Why Conservatives Are Going Nuclear on Pope Francis,"
The Week, September 22, 2015, http://theweek.com/articles/578428/
why-conservatives-are-going-nuclear-pope-francis.

30. William Saletan, "The Patron Saint of the Left: Why Pope Francis Isn't the
Liberal Rock Star American Catholics Think He Is," *Slate*, September 20,
2015, http://www.slate.com/articles/news_and_politics/politics/2015/09/

pope_francis_in_the_united_states_why_he_isn_t_the_liberal_rock_star_american.html.

31. Kathleen Geier, "Pope Francis Is Not a Feminist: Why Catholicism's Liberal Icon Falls Far Short on Women's Issues," *Salon*, July 26, 2015, http://www.salon.com/2015/07/26/pope_francis_is_not_a_feminist_why_catholicisms_liberal_icon_falls_far_short_on_womens_issues/.

32. Pope Francis, *Laudato Sí*, 23.

33. Pope Francis, *Laudato Sí*, 51.

34. Pope Francis, "Laudato Si—chapter one, What is happening to our Common Home," *Crux*, June 18, 2015, 61, http://www.cruxnow.com/church/2015/06/18/laudato-si-chapter-one-what-is-happening-to-our-common-home/.

35. Pope Francis, Address to members of the diplomatic corps, Sala Regia, January 8, 2009, http://w2.vatican.va/content/benedict-xvi/en/speeches/2009/january/documents/hf_ben-xvi_spe_20090108_diplomatic-corps.html.

36. Pope John Paul II, *Ecclesia in Oceania*, November 22, 2001, http://w2.vatican.va/content/john-paul-ii/en/apost_exhortations/documents/hf_jp-ii_exh_20011122_ecclesia-in-oceania.html.

37. Pope Francis, *Laudato Sí*, 222.

38. Pope Francis, *Laudato Sí*, 108.

CHAPTER NINE

1. "Attorney General Lynch Announces Federal Marriage Benefits Available to Same-Sex Couples Nationwide," U.S. Department of Justice, July 9, 2015, http://www.justice.gov/opa/pr/attorney-general-lynch-announces-federal-marriage-benefits-available-same-sex-couples.

2. Nash Jenkins, "Hundreds Gather for Unveiling of Satanic Statue in Detroit", *Time*, July 27, 2015, http://time.com/3972713/detroit-satanic-statue-baphomet/.

3. Devin Leonard "It's Amazon's World. The USPS Just Delivers in It," *Bloomberg Businessweek*, July 30, 2015, http://www.bloomberg.com/news/articles/2015-07-30/it-s-amazon-s-world-the-usps-just-delivers-in-it.

4. A. Pawlowski, "'It felt like she was the boss': How to Deal with Kids Who Bully Their Parents," *Today*, July 28, 2015, http://www.today.com/parents/why-children-bully-parents-how-regain-control-t34996.

5. There were nine videos released between July 14, 2015 and October 27, 2015. "Investigative Footage," Center for Medical Progress,, http://www.centerformedicalprogress.org/cmp/investigative-footage/.

6. Simon Thomsen, "Extramarital Affair Website Ashley Madison Has Been Hacked and Attackers Are Threatening to Leak Data Online," *Business Insider*, July 20, 2015, http://www.businessinsider.com/cheating-affair-website-ashley-madison-hacked-user-data-leaked-2015-7.

7. "Cardinal George—Keep Conscience Protections for Health Care Workers," YouTube video, United States Conference of Catholic Bishops, March 16,

2009, https://youtu.be/6NoCRwMqVzQ.

8. *Testimony of Most Reverend William E. Lori Bishop of Bridgeport on behalf of the United States Conference of Catholic Bishops Before the Judiciary Committee of the United States House of Representatives, Subcommittee on the Constitution,* October 26, 2011, http://www.usccb.org/issues-and-action/religious-liberty/upload/lori-testimony-on-religious-freedom-2011-10-26.pdf.

9. Cardinal Francis George, OMI, "The Wrong Side of History," *Catholic New World,* October 21–November 3, 2012, http://www.catholicnewworld.com/cnwonline/2012/1021/cardinal.aspx.

10. "Must Religious Bakers Bake Cakes for Gay Weddings?" *The Economist,* July 16, 2015, http://www.economist.com/blogs/democracyinamerica/2015/07/gay-rights-and-religious-freedom.

11. See the opinion by Justice Anthony Kennedy in Obergefell et al. v. Hodgeset al., 576 U.S. (2015), p. 27, http://www.supremecourt.gov/opinions/14pdf/14-556_3204.pdf.

12. Chief Justice John Roberts, Dissenting, Obergefell et al. v. Hodgeset al., 576 U.S. (2015), p. 28, http://www.supremecourt.gov/opinions/14pdf/14-556_3204.pdf.

13. "Pope Francis is Welcomed at the White House," *Aleteia,* September 23, 2015, http://aleteia.org/2015/09/23/pope-francis-is-welcomed-at-the-white-house/.

14. Pope Francis, White House Welcoming Ceremony, South Lawn of the White House, Washington, D.C., September 23, 2015, https://w2.vatican.va/content/francesco/en/speeches/2015/september/documents/papa-francesco_20150923_usa-benvenuto.html (emphasis added).

15. "Frequently Asked Questions: Little Sisters of the Poor," The Becket Fund for Religious Liberty, accessed February 2, 2016, http://www.becketfund.org/faqlittlesistersofthepoor/.

16. Elizabeth Chuck and Tracy Connor, "Pope Francis Visits Little Sisters of the Poor, Nuns in Obamacare Lawsuit," *NBC News,* September 24, 2015, http://www.nbcnews.com/storyline/pope-francis-visits-america/spiritual-shot-arm-pope-visits-nuns-obamacare-suit-n432931.

17. Dan Zak, "Meet Yayo Grassi, the Gay Man Who Is Friends with Pope Francis," *The Washington Post,* October 2, 2015, https://www.washingtonpost.com/news/acts-of-faith/wp/2015/10/02/meet-yayo-grassi-the-gay-man-who-is-friends-with-pope-francis/.

18. Ryan Anderson, "We Don't Need Kim Davis to Be in Jail," *The New York Times,* September 7, 2015, http://www.nytimes.com/2015/09/07/opinion/we-dont-need-kim-davis-to-be-in-jail.html.

19. Jim Yardley and Laurie Goodstein, "Pope Francis Met with Kim Davis, Kentucky County Clerk, in Washington," *The New York Times,* September 30, 2015, http://www.nytimes.com/2015/09/30/us/county-clerk-kim-davis-who-denied-gay-couples-visited-pope.html.

20. "Kim Davis Recounts Secret Meeting with Pope Francis," *ABC News*, September 30, 2015, http://abcnews.go.com/US/exclusive-kim-davis-recounts-secret-meeting-pope-francis/story?id=34143874.

21. Vatican Radio, "Holy See Press Office issues statement on Pope's meeting with Kim Davis," News.va, October 2, 2015, http://www.news.va/en/news/holy-see-press-office-issues-statement-on-popes-me.

22. "Pope Francis: "I'm not a star, but the servant of servants of God," Vatican Radio, September 28, 2015, http://en.radiovaticana.va/news/2015/09/28/pope_francis_i%E2%80%99m_not_a_star,_but_the_servant_of_servants_o/1175317.

23. Pope Francis, Visit to the joint session of the United States Congress, United States Capitol, Washington, D.C., September 24, 2015, https://w2.vatican.va/content/francesco/en/speeches/2015/september/documents/papa-francesco_20150924_usa-us-congress.html.

24. Pope Francis, Meeting with the Members of the General Assembly of the United Nations Organization, United Nations Headquarters, New York, September 25, 2015, http://w2.vatican.va/content/francesco/en/speeches/2015/september/documents/papa-francesco_20150925_onu-visita.html.

25. John Lennon, "Imagine," *Imagine*, Apple Corps Ltd./Capitol Records, 1971.

26. Pope Francis, Meeting for Religious Liberty with the Hispanic Community and Other Immigrants, Independence Mall, Philadelphia, September 26, 2015, http://w2.vatican.va/content/francesco/en/speeches/2015/september/documents/papa-francesco_20150926_usa-liberta-religiosa.html.

27. Pope Francis, Holy Mass and Canonization of Blessed Fr. Junipero Serra, National Shrine of the Immaculate Conception, Washington, D.C., September 23, 2015, http://w2.vatican.va/content/francesco/en/homilies/2015/documents/papa-francesco_20150923_usa-omelia-washington-dc.html.

28. John L. Allen Jr., "Pope Francis lays out gentle critique of Cuba's Socialist revolution," *Crux*, September 20, 2015.

29. Pope Francis, In-Flight Press Conference from Santiago de Cuba, September 22, 2015, http://w2.vatican.va/content/francesco/en/speeches/2015/september/documents/papa-francesco_20150922_intervista-santiago-washington.html.

30. Pope Francis, Greeting to the organizing committee, volunteers and benefactors, Philadelphia International Airport, September 27, 2015, http://w2.vatican.va/content/francesco/en/speeches/2015/september/documents/papa-francesco_20150927_usa-comitato-organizzatore.html.

31. Pope Francis, Meeting for Religious Liberty.

32. "Pope Francis' Impromptu Speech at Festival of Families in Philadelphia Transcript," *Our Sunday Visitor*, September 27, 2015. https://www.osv.com/OSVNewsweekly/PapalVisit/Articles/Article/TabId/2727/ArtMID/20933/ArticleID/18334/Pope-Francis-impromptu-speech-at-Festival-of-Families-in-Philadelphia.aspx.

33. Pope Francis, White House Welcoming Ceremony.

34. "Pope's Address to Bishops from Around the World Attending Meeting of Families," *Zenit*, September 28, 2015, http://zenit.org/articles/pope-s-address-to-bishops-from-around-the-world-attending-meeting-of-families/.

CHAPTER TEN

1. Eric Garland, "Boehner's Most Emotional Pope Moment That No One Saw," *The Hill*, September 25, 2015.

2. Robert Costa, "What John Boehner Told Me the Night Before He Said He Was Quitting," *The Washington Post*, September 25, 2015.

3. Tom Hoopes, "Raven on Hand for Little Sisters of the Poor Meeting," The Gregorian (blog), September 30, 2015, http://www.thegregorian.org/blog/raven-on-hand-for-little-sisters-of-the-poor-meeting.

4. Nichole Winfield and David Crary, "Pope Francis Mingles with High and Low in New York visit," Associated Press, September 25, 2015, http://bigstory.ap.org/article/47dee60b9f1547c08454997d9ec1c6a5/pope-francis-set-bring-his-message-world-leaders-un.

5. Michael Wilson, "Pope Francis, in New York, Takes on Extremism and Inequality," *The New York Times*, September 25, 2015, http://www.nytimes.com/2015/09/26/nyregion/pope-francis-visits-new-york-city.html.

6. "Pope's Visit Restores Hope to a Woman at Ground Zero on 9-11," *Aleteia*, September 26, 2015, http://aleteia.org/2015/09/26/popes-visit-restores-hope-to-a-woman-at-ground-zero-on-9-11/.

7. Jonathan Liedl, "Bishops Encouraged by Pope Francis' Words," *National Catholic Register*, September 25, 2015, https://www.ncregister.com/daily-news/bishops-encouraged-by-pope-francis-words.

8. Matt Hadro, "How the Pope Used the Environment to Preach to the U.N.," Catholic News Agency, September 25, 2015, http://www.catholicnewsagency.com/news/how-the-pope-used-the-environment-to-preach-to-the-un-12859/.

9. Pope Francis, Homily, Madison Square Garden, September 25, 2015, https://w2.vatican.va/content/francesco/en/homilies/2015/documents/papa-francesco_20150925_usa-omelia-nyc.html.

10. "Pope's Address to Bishops from Around the World."

11. Pope Francis, Meeting with Young People from Argentina, Rio de Janeiro, July 25, 2013, https://w2.vatican.va/content/francesco/en/speeches/2013/july/documents/papa-francesco_20130725_gmg-argentini-rio.html.

12. Pope Francis, *The Name of God Is Mercy*, 99.

13. Pope Francis, Evangelii Gaudium, 288.

MORE INSPIRATIONAL READING ON
POPE FRANCIS

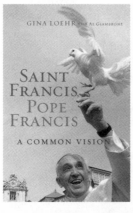
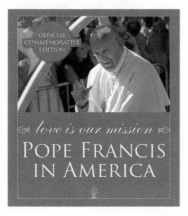